World War II
The Pacific War

The MILITARY HISTORY of the UNITED STATES

Christopher Chant

World War II
The Pacific War

MARSHALL CAVENDISH
NEW YORK · LONDON · TORONTO · SYDNEY

Library Edition Published 1992

Published by
Marshall Cavendish Corporation
2415 Jerusalem Avenue.
PO Box 587
North Bellmore
New York 11710

Series created by Graham Beehag Book Design

Series Editor	Maggi McCormick
Consultant Editors	James R. Arnold
	Roberta Wiener
Sub Editor	Julie Cairns
Designer	Graham Beehag
Illustrators	John Batchelor
	Steve Lucas
	Terry Forest
	Colette Brownrigg
Indexer	Mark Dartford

Library of Congress Cataloging-in-Publication Data

Chant, Christopher.
The Military History of the United States / Christopher Chant – Library ed.
p. cm.
Includes bibliographical references and index.
Summary: Surveys the wars that have directly influenced the United States., from the Revolutionary War through the Cold War.
ISBN 1-85435-361-6 ISBN 1-85435-361-9 (set)
1. United States - History, Military - Juvenile literature.
[1. United States - History, Military.] I. Title.
t181.C52 1991
973 - dc20 90 - 19547
CIP
AC

Printed in Singapore by Times Offset PTE Ltd
Bound in the United States

The publishers wish to thank the following organizations who have supplied photographs:

The National Archives, Washington. United States Navy, United States Marines, United States Army, United States Air Force, Department of Defense, Library of Congress, The Smithsonian Institution.

The publishers gratefully thank the U.S. Army Military History Institute, Carlisle Barracks, PA. for the use of archive material for the following witness accounts:

Page 14-17
From papers donated by Lieutenant Colonel Denver D. Gray, 17 Service Group, Air Corps, 1942. Also, interviews with Bataan Death March Survivors, 192nd Battalion, conducted by the Kentucky Historical Society, 1961.

Page 95

Defending the Driniumor Covering Force Operations in New Guinea, 1944 by Edward Drea (Fort Leavenworth, 1984).

Contents

Limited Objectives, Not All-Out War 7
Balanced Forces 9
The Attack on Pearl Harbor 12
Nagumo's Fatal Error 13
The Epic Defense of Wake Island 17
Strategic Importance of the Philippines 18
Disaster at Clark Field 20
The Japanese Land in Lingayen Gulf 21
MacArthur Leaves the Philippines 23
The Japanese Advance into the East Indies 24
American Naval Involvement 25
The "Doolittle Raid" 28
The Battle of the Coral Sea 30
The Battle of Midway Starts with Japanese Success 33
A Total Disaster for the Japanese 34
Loss of the *Yorktown* 35
One of History's Most Decisive Battles 36
The Invasion of Guadalcanal 42
The Battle of Bloody Ridge 44
The Battle of Savo Island 46
The Battle of the Eastern Solomons 47
The Battle of Cape Esperance 49
The Battle of the Santa Cruz Islands 50
The Battle of Guadalcanal 53
The Battles of Tassafaronga and Rennell's Island 54
Operations in New Guinea 55
The Battle for Buna and Gona 56
MacArthur's Renewed Offensive 58
The Battle of the Bismarck Sea 59
The Role of Tactical Air Power 61
First Landings on New Britain 62
The Death of Yamamoto 65
Operation "Toenails" 65
Operation "Cherryblossom" 71
The Battle of Kula Gulf 71
The Battles of Kolombangara and Vella Gulf 72
The Battle of Vella Lavella 72
The Battle of Empress Augusta Bay 72
Japanese Defeat in the Aleutians 74
Buildup in the Central Pacific Area 75
Capture of the Marshalls 76
Bloody Tarawa 79
The Capture of Kwajalein 83
Reduction of Eniwetok 84
MacArthur's Strategic Masterstroke 90
Complete Success in New Guinea 91
The Battle of the Philippine Sea 96
"The Great Marianas Turkey Shoot" 102
Approach to the Philippines 107
The Landing on Leyte 109
The Battle of the Sibuyan Sea 111
The Battle of Surigao Strait 112
The Battle off Samar 113
The Battle off Cape Engano 113
Bloody Fighting for Iwo Jima 116
The Okinawa Campaign 119
Strategic Bombing of Japan 123
Atom Bombings End World War II 131

Glossary 132
Bibliography 134
Index 135

Early in 1940, Japan altered the nature of her war in China. Her original policy – of outright military victory – was revised. Instead, she would throttle China economically; this would take longer, but at the same time would free men and materiel for other tasks The primary objective was to take the so-called Southern Resources Area, which included Southeast Asia (Thailand, French Indochina, and the British possessions of Burma and Malaya) and the British, Dutch, and Portuguese possessions in the East Indies. The area offered a wide variety of strategically important raw materials, and though Japan preferred a peaceful penetration of the area she was prepared to take it by force.

A minor U.S. embargo on exports to Japan imposed in January 1940 was intended to serve as a small-scale warning, but Japan was not deterred. Then the success of Germany's Western European campaign in May and June 1940 completely upset the balance of power in Southeast Asia. France and the Netherlands had been defeated, and the United Kingdom had been pushed close to defeat. Japan was left with an essentially free hand in the Pacific area. The Southern Resources Area was there for the taking if the United States could be dissuaded or prevented from intervening.

The Greater East Asia Co-Prosperity Sphere

In July 1940, a new cabinet dominated by the military set Japan's objective in the area: the establishment of the so-called Greater East Asia Co-Prosperity Sphere, which added New Guinea and the Philippines to the Southern Resources Area. The planned preliminaries for a move in this direction were ending hostilities in China, a closer alignment with Germany and Italy (achieved in September

One key to successful aircraft carrier operations was having the right number of the right type of aircraft. Seen here on the flight deck of the *Saratoga* after May 1942 are two of the U.S. Navy's best warplanes of the first part of the war, namely the Grumman F4F Wildcat fighter (coded 3-F-15 in the right foreground) and the Douglas SBD Dauntless dive-bomber.

One of the most striking features of World War II in the Pacific Ocean was the effect of air power. As a result, the light antiaircraft defenses of American and Japanese ships were strengthened enormously during the course of the war so that a wall of fire could be thrown into the air in the path of attackers. In the battleship *North Carolina*, for example, the original battery of sixteen 1.1-in guns was eventually replaced by ninety-six 40-mm Bofors guns. Another important weapon was the dual-purpose 5-in gun, generally located in a twin turret and used for antiship/shore and antiaircraft purposes. Seen during firing practice, this is one of the 5-in twin turrets on the "Cleveland" class light cruiser *Biloxi*, which carried six such turrets in addition to twelve 6-in guns in four triple turrets. The ships of this large and important class also carried either twenty-four or twenty-eight 40-mm Bofors guns.

1940), and a non-aggression pact with the U.S.S.R. (signed in April 1941). Japan moved troops into Indochina during September 1940. At the same time, she tried without success to pressure the Dutch government in exile to allocate virtually all the oil production of the Dutch East Indies to Japan.

The Japanese realized that war was probable rather than possible when the United States froze Japanese assets, thereby imposing a total trade embargo, during July 1941. Some Japanese leaders urged that agreement should be reached with the United States, but the leaders of the army were confident that Japan had adequate reserves of oil and that Japan should not back down. While talks continued in Washington, Japan's military and naval leaders sat down to the task of creating a comprehensive strategy for the imminent war.

Limited Objectives, Not All-Out War

This conflict was never planned as an all-out war with the United States. It was intended to gain limited objectives. The war's first phase, expected to last five months, included a surprise attack to neutralize the U.S. Navy's Pacific Fleet. This strike would prevent U.S. interference with Japan's other military operations, the seizure of the Greater East Asia Co-Prosperity Sphere, and the capture of other areas considered essential to defend the perimeter that was to be created around the Greater East Asia Co-Prosperity Sphere. The war's second phase involved consolidating and strengthening this defensive perimeter. Third, the perimeter would be defended against any forces attempting to break through it.

Japan's military leaders thought that the United States would shy away from the manpower and materiel costs of the long operations that would be needed to break through this perimeter. Therefore, they would reach an accommodation permitting Japan to retain her conquests.

As this plan, together with detailed schemes for its implementation, was being evolved, negotiations continued through the summer and fall of 1941. Neither side would compromise, and the result was a frustrated lack of progress. The army and navy emphasized to

Washington D.C.
For further references see pages 11, 23, *37*

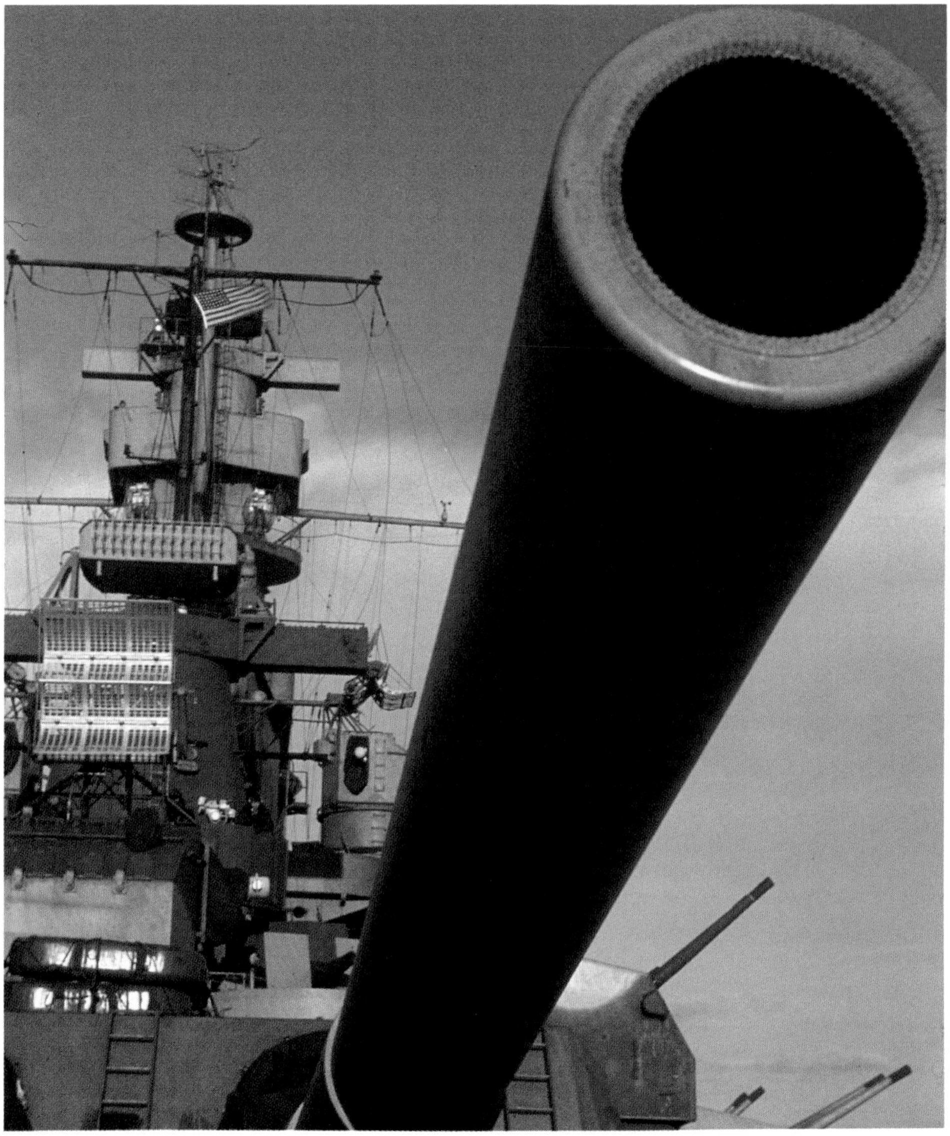

A close-up view of one of the nine 16-in guns carried in three triple turrets by the *Alabama*, one of four "South Dakota" class battleships. The ships were comparatively short and therefore more maneuverable than other American battleships. When they were fitted with radar fire-control equipment of the type visible behind the turret, they could deliver devastatingly accurate fire against ship and shore targets.

the Japanese cabinet that the growing shortage of raw materials was beginning to limit Japan's options. Prince Konoye, the prime minister, wanted to extend the October 15 deadline that his cabinet had earlier set as the deadline for negotiations, and to offer the United States a Japanese withdrawal from China. The Japanese army refused, and Konoye's government fell. General Hideki Tojo became prime minister of the new government formed on October 18.

An American Ultimatum?

On November 5, this government agreed to continue negotiations until November 25 (later extended to November 29), and made a conditional offer to pull Japanese forces out of China. The United States felt that acceptance of these Japanese conditions would condone Japan's initial aggression and therefore refused the offer. On November 26, Secretary of State Cordell Hull told the Japanese negotiators that the United States demanded not just a Japanese withdrawal from China and recognition of Generalissimo Chiang Kai-shek's Nationalist government, but also the evacuation of Japanese forces from French Indochina.

Japan regarded this as a wholly unacceptable American ultimatum and continued negotiations only as a ploy to gain time and the element of strategic surprise. Final preparations for war now started in earnest. By November 6, Japan's most senior military and naval commanders had been instructed to prepare detailed plans within the context of Japan's overall strategy. On November 25, the 1st Air Fleet sailed from Hitokappu Bay in the Kurile Islands north of the Japanese home islands. The 1st Air Fleet's destination was the Hawaiian Islands.

On December 1, the Japanese set December 8 (December 7 east of the international date line) as the day for the beginning of hostilities.

Balanced Forces

The Imperial Japanese navy could muster 11 battleships and battle cruisers, 11 aircraft carriers, 18 heavy cruisers (with guns of 8-inch caliber or more), 23 light cruisers (with guns of 6-inch caliber or less), 129 destroyers, and 67 submarines. Against this arsenal, the Allies would be able to call on 11 battleships and battle cruisers (nine American and two British), three aircraft carriers (all American), 14 heavy cruisers (13 American and one British), 21 light cruisers (11 American, seven British, and three Dutch), 100 destroyers (80 American, 13 British, and seven Dutch), and 69 submarines (56 American and 13 Dutch). In everything but aircraft carriers, the two sides were therefore matched fairly evenly. But the Japanese had overwhelming advantages: a single command structure, superior carrierborne aircraft and combat-experienced pilots, and ships, which were generally newer, faster, and more heavily armed than the Allied ships.

U.S. strength in the Pacific included the Pacific and Asiatic Fleets; in the Atlantic, for possible use against Germany and Italy, was the Atlantic Fleet with eight battleships, four aircraft carriers, five heavy cruisers, eight light cruisers, 93 destroyers, and 56 submarines.

In December 1941, the Imperial Japanese army had 51 divisions and 59 independent brigades. Only ten divisions and four brigades were allocated to the four armies entrusted with offensive operations. The remaining formations were retained in Japan, Manchuria, China, and Indochina for use as needed. To secure its main objective the Japanese capture of the Southern Resources Area also meant that the Pacific Fleet must be neutralized and the Philippines seized.

Japan's Basic Plan

The sequence of principal events was based upon a surprise air attack on Pearl Harbor, followed almost immediately by air attacks on the main Allied air bases in the Philippines and Malaya. The Philippines and Malaya were then invaded as the first steps in the two-pronged advance into the East Indies. Secondary moves at the same time included the occupation of Thailand, the seizures of Hong Kong, Guam in the Mariana islands, and Wake Island north of the Marshall Islands. Just a few days later, the British possession of Sarawak on the northwestern side of Borneo was invaded.

A chief petty officer at his station in the control room of an American submarine. Operating from the main base at Pearl Harbor, the American submarine fleet was destined to play a major part in the naval war in the Pacific. The success of these boats decimated Japan's merchant navy, which curtailed Japan's ability to move raw materials to Japan, and men plus their equipment from Japan. The boats also shadowed major Japanese surface forces, relaying position and strength information, and picking off ships whenever possible.

In their overall concept, the Japanese plans were professional and thorough. No unified command was set up, however, and the major army and navy forces were merely instructed to cooperate.

The idea for the attack on Pearl Harbor was first conceived in January 1941 by the commander-in-chief of the Combined Fleet, Admiral Isoroku Yamamoto, who drew his inspiration for the attack in November 1940 in which the Royal Navy's Fleet Air Arm had crippled major elements of the Italian fleet in Taranto harbor. Yamamoto's scheme was so bold that at first it scared naval planners, and it was worked into the final Japanese plan only during October. Convinced that it was essential, Yamamoto had meanwhile refined the original concept, gathered the right personnel, implemented a program of thorough training, and gathered intelligence about the Pacific Fleet and Pearl Harbor. So the 1st Air Fleet was completely ready when it was alerted in mid-November as the core of the Pearl Harbor Strike Force.

The Decisive Instrument

Commanded by Vice Admiral Chuichi Nagumo, the 1st Air Fleet was based on six modern aircraft carriers with 414 aircraft. Its other ships were one light cruiser and nine destroyers. Heavy support was provided by two battleships and two heavy cruisers, and the fleet train included eight tankers and supply ships. The fleet sailed from the Kuriles across the northern Pacific. Although this route increased the difficulty of refuelling at sea in the prevailing poor weather and sea conditions, it significantly reduced the possibility of American or even neutral shipping and aircraft spotting and reporting the Japanese ships.

By 6:00 a.m., exactly on schedule, the 1st Air Fleet arrived at the position, 200 miles north of Oahu, from which it was to launch its two waves of attack aircraft. Since November 26, the American political and military leadership had become aware of the Japanese preparations for war, but American intelligence suggested that the target for these preparations was either the Philippines or Malaya. American intelligence had broken the secret radio code used by the Japanese navy and was therefore aware of the location and movements of most Japanese warships. The 1st Air Fleet had sailed under strict radio silence, however, leaving radios in Japanese waters to simulate the traffic of its ships. The U.S. was therefore completely unaware of the 1st Air Fleet's position just north of the Hawaiian Islands.

Since the U.S. had adopted the "Germany first" policy in January 1941, the American forces in the Pacific Ocean

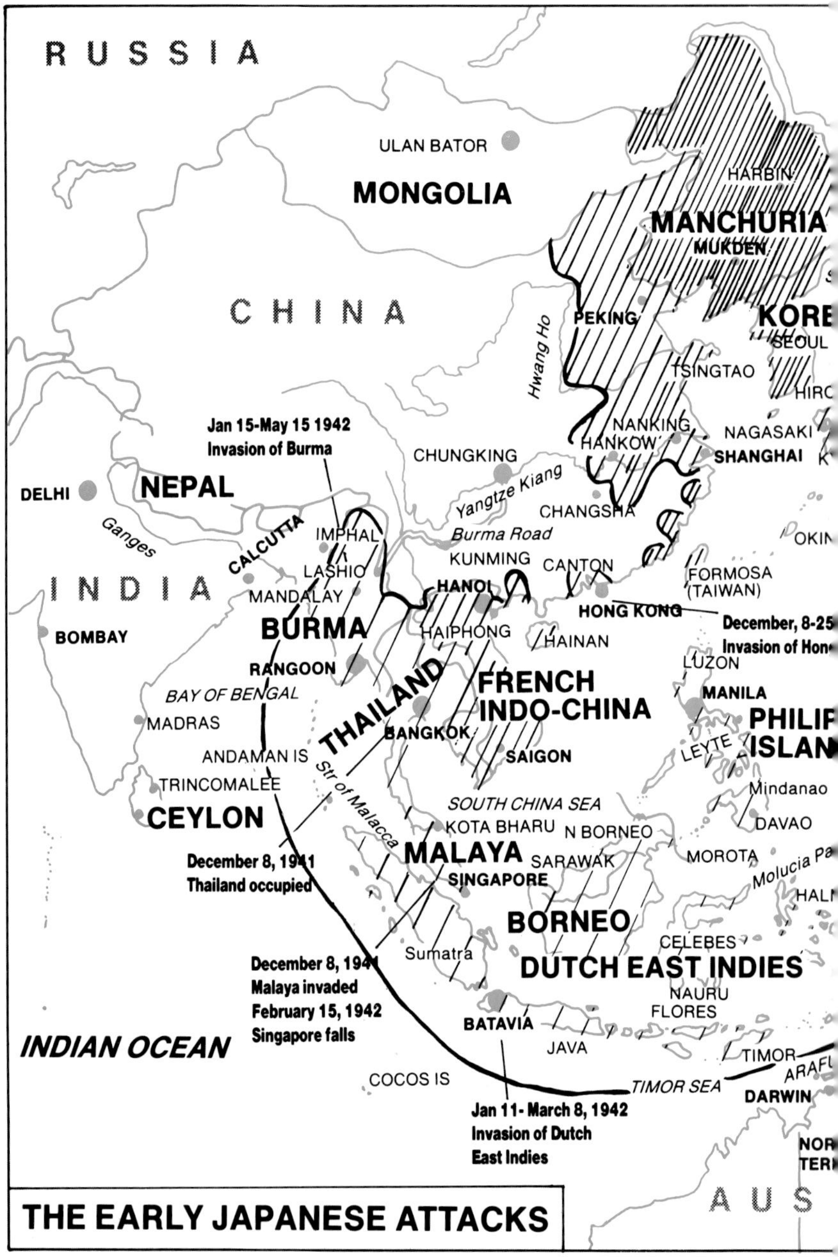

Japan's tide of expansion continued up to August 1942, but was checked in the Battles of the Coral Sea and Midway.

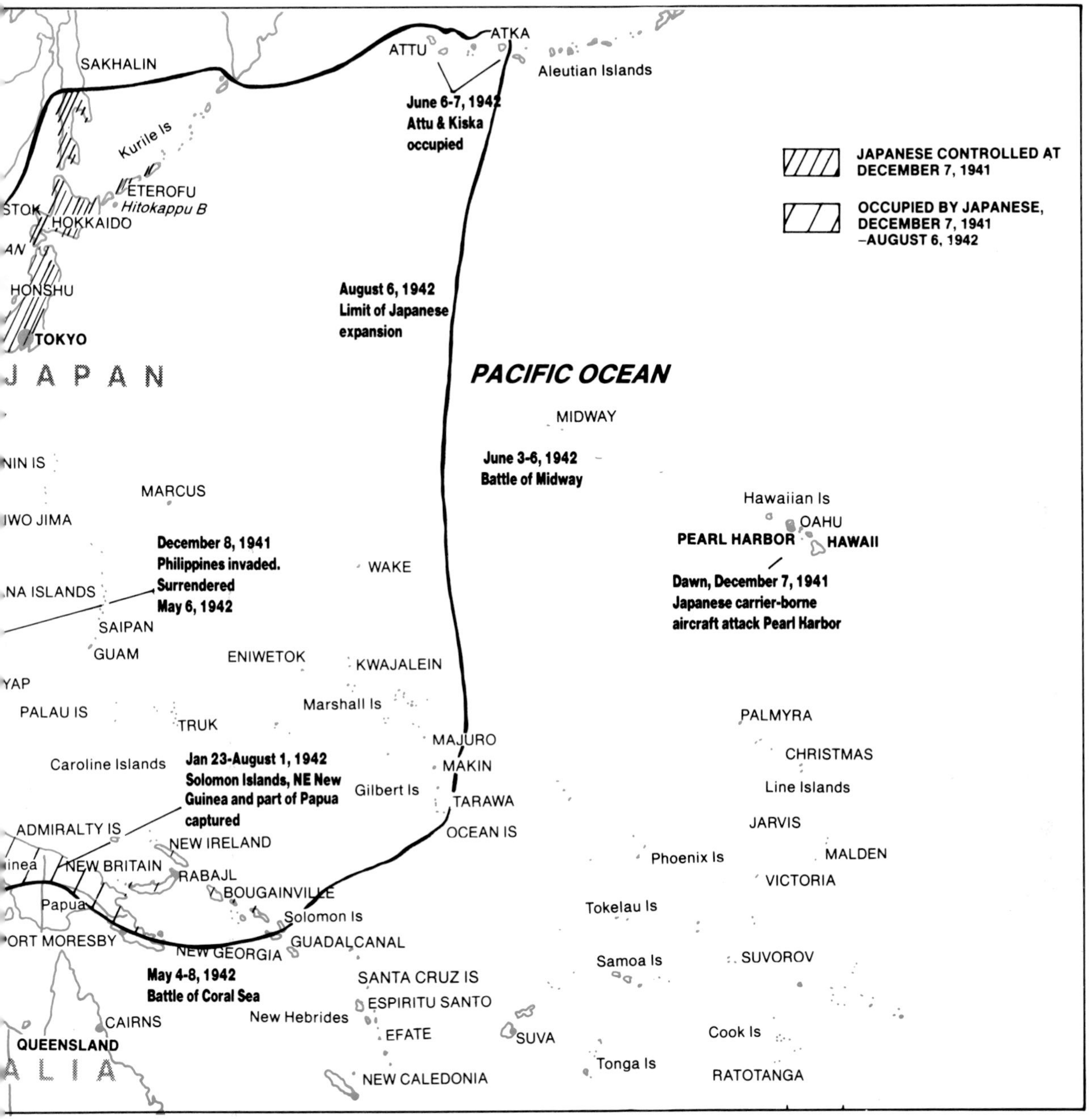

areas had been given a purely defensive role. According to the current "Rainbow 5" overall strategic plan, the Philippines would be defended, but would receive no reinforcement. The Marshall Islands would be captured to provide U.S. forces with bases for subsequent offensive operations to the west.

The core of the American defense posture was the Hawaiian Islands, which were to be held as the main base for all U.S. operations in the Pacific. In December 1941, the islands were the joint responsibility of the army and navy commanders, Lieutenant General Walter C. Short and Admiral Husband E. Kimmel. They had to implement the local defense plan, which depended on close cooperation between the two services. In December 1941, cooperation was far from perfect. Shortages of trained personnel and equipment meant that neither the radar warning system nor the system of warning air patrols was very effective.

The two commanders had been warned on November 27 that war with Japan was imminent, but neither put his forces on full war alert. Washington sent

Pearl Harbor
For further references see pages *9*, 10, 13, 14, 17, 19, 28, 32, 35, 105, 113

additional, but somewhat vague, information about a possible attack before December 7, but still the defenses were not readied.

The Attack on Pearl Harbor

December 7 was a Sunday, and the U.S. forces were in an almost holiday mood as the decisive moment approached. There were a few niggling worries such as submarine sightings and a radar report of massed aircraft, but they failed to penetrate the complacency of the day. Except for the three aircraft carriers, which were fortunately absent from Pearl Harbor, the Pacific Fleet was a sitting target. It rode neatly at anchor in just the fashion indicated by Japanese intelligence. At the same time, aircraft on all of Oahu's seven airfields were located in close-packed rows. This formation made it more difficult for saboteurs, who were thought to be the greatest threat, to attack.

The skill of the Japanese planning was matched by the excellence with which the attack was carried out. The first wave of Japanese aircraft, 45 Mitsubishi A6M Zero fighters escorting 54 Aichi D3A dive-bombers and 90 Nakajima B5N bombers, (40 torpedo bombers and 50 level bombers carrying armor-piercing naval shells fitted with fins to serve as bombs), took off at 6:00 a.m. The initial report of this formation at 7:00 a.m. was discounted, and the Japanese aircraft which arrived over northern Oahu at 7:40 a.m. had complete surprise as they swung southwest over the island to attack from the northwest and west. The fighters found no aerial opposition and therefore broke away to strafe the aircraft on all airfields except the one at Haleiwa, while the bombers tore into the Pacific Fleet's ships. By 8.25 a.m., the first

The greatest single disaster on the ill-starred day of December 7, 1941, was the loss of the battleship *Arizona*, seen here with smoke billowing upward from her many fires following the Japanese attack.

Tangled wreckage at a U.S. Army air base after the Japanese raids on Oahu.

wave had completed its task and was heading back to the Japanese carriers.

A few American aircraft had now gotten into the sky, but they were generally massacred as the second wave of Japanese attack aircraft swept over them. This wave, including 31 fighters, 81 dive-bombers, and 54 level bombers, completed the work started by the first wave even though all the bombers carried comparatively light bombs for attacks on the absent aircraft carriers. The Japanese aircraft arrived off northeastern Oahu shortly after 8:50 a.m. and attacked from the north and east. By 9:45 a.m., the last Japanese aircraft had gone, leaving a scene of total devastation.

Of the Pacific Fleet's eight battleships, three had been sunk, another capsized, and another three so seriously damaged that they would be out of action for months. The Pacific Fleet also lost three light cruisers, three destroyers, and several other vessels sunk or seriously damaged. On land, the Japanese had destroyed 188 and damaged 159 of 394 first-line aircraft. Of the Army Air Forces' 231 miscellaneous machines, 166 remained intact or were reparable; only 54 of the Navy's 250 miscellaneous aircraft survived intact or reparable.

Despite their surprise, the men of the U.S. Army, Navy, and Marine Corps had fought back with great determination, suffering 2,403 killed (226 soldiers and 2,177 sailors) and 1,178 wounded (396 soldiers and 782 sailors).

Nagumo's Fatal Error

The Japanese airmen escaped virtually unscathed, losing only 29 aircraft and their crews. Other losses included six Japanese submarines, five of them midget boats. The commanders of the Japanese naval air units, all middle-ranking officers, urged Nagumo to launch a third attack wave to destroy the Pacific Fleet's port facilities, including the all-important repair yards and oil storage tanks. Knowing that the Americans were now fully alerted and might handle any such attack severely, and fearing that the position of his carriers might have been deduced and be attracting an American attack, Nagumo refused to allow a third attack. It proved to be a decisive mistake.

Pearl Harbor was a major disaster, but was salvaged from becoming a national calamity by the absence of the three carriers. The U.S.S. *Lexington* and U.S.S.

Chuichi Nagumo
For further references see pages 10, 32, 33, 34, 46, 95, 96

An American radio intelligence unit listened to and translated the following broadcast describing the Japanese attack on Pearl Harbour.

We at last received the order which we had so anxiously waited for . . . the order to attack the island of Oahu. The thing which had to happen had at last come. Our mental attitude was calm . . . We reconciled ourselves to all which lay ahead.

We lined up on deck, in our hearts . . . a solemn promise to the Emperor. Here would be decided the destiny of the Empire. Moved to the extreme was each and every individual. All was silent . . . for now indeed on the Pacific would be repeated the epoch-making 40 years' history following the Russo-Japanese war. We accepted our orders and saluted. "We're ready. We'll see it through." This was the resolute determination. As long as we live, never will we forget the moment when the signal flag was silently dropped.

Immediately, our squadron set out. Full speed for Hawaii!

Responsibility lay on each one of us. We had made necessary preparations. We had plenty of rest.

At last on the morning of the sixth, or 7th by Hawaii time we were ordered to start out. One by one our planes soared off the deck glistening in the sunlight.

In a short while, Oahu lay below us. The enemy air field is right under us. The whole squadron was ordered to turn. We at once fell in to attack according to our duties.

Leading a group of large bombers, I skirted the island on the west side, and suddenly moved into the attack. Pearl Harbor lies as though inviting us. The sighter takes accurate aim. The machine gunner peers.

As the order for attack comes our souls are even more determined. Because of our training we are all a single unit.

All at once we looked down. There is an outburst below. From the middle of an enemy ship a huge column of water rises. It was a well-aimed shot, an admirable shot. Four, then five aerial torpedoes are released which find their mark.

Though only three or five minutes passed, I had to wait until the initial attack ended. Enemy fighter planes have not yet risen. Anti-aircraft guns have not yet fired. Hawaii is still asleep. There is no response from the stricken enemy ships. With the first assault successful, we send off a wireless message.

Next our bombers come down from above the clouds. In no time at all the planes at the airport are enveloped in black smoke. As we prepare for our second attack and meet new targets, at last the enemy's anti-aircraft shells begin to burst around us. Next is the baptism of the large bombers. I was at the head of the last file of planes. The air current was very bad. I released but two bundles of bombs as the aim was poor. We have to try to destroy the hangers again. The fighter planes behind us and another squadron behind us also have to try again.

This time we're successful. As we look behind, flames are roaring some 500 meters heavenward. We had hit the enemy's powder magazines.

One of the enemy ships has exploded. The entire ship is in flames. Oil is set afires. That ship must have been of the Arizona class.

We all shout "Banzai"!

At Wheeler airport more fighter planes and light bombers are assembled. As they are bombed, they all burn and set off billows of black smoke.

Now we change our course for the second attack on Pearl Harbor. There are still two battleships side by side in Pearl Harbor. We divide into two groups and each attack one ship. They are easy prey. The first bomber dives in. The others stand by. As one bomber passes over, a column of water and splinters rises some 50 to 100 meters in the air. For this reason the next machine must wait an interval. The attack lasts along while because of these waits. Nevertheless, we proceed with a thorough attack.

The order which we received before we

ew is now being carried out before my eyes.

As we prepare to leave, we can see two battleships sinking. Another is sinking at a 45 degree angle. The ship which was attacked first is now underneath burning oil. Three more ships are flaming. The American Fleet has been crushed.

The early morning sun was now shining brightly. When we returned to our ship, the second attack group was leaving.

An American survivor, Ensign George B. Lennig, of the *Arizona* describes what it was like to be victim of the surprise Japanese attack:

I was asleep in my room located in the Lower Ward Room about eight frames aft of the athwartships armored bulkhead on the third deck. I awakened upon the passing of the word, "All hands man your General Quarters Stations!!" and had commenced dressing when I heard a violent explosion somewhere forward. The lights went out on both the normal lighting circuit and the battle circuit. I completed dressing and started forward and up the ladder to the second deck when a very close and violent explosion sent flame and burning debris down the ladder. After falling back for a moment, I ascended to the second deck and found the smoke and fire, caused by a bomb hit outside the Captain's Cabin, too dense to pass through. I went to the foot of the ladder and connected the fire hose, but there was no pressure. This failing, I soaked a towel in the waste water bucket under the basin in my room and proceeded up and forward to find that the oil-covered water was now rushing into the second deck from what appeared to be forward. I attempted to drop the hatch to the lower Ward Room Country but was able to loosen only one supporting bar. By this time, the water was waist deep on the second deck with the lower Ward Room Country filling rapidly.

I heard an intermittent screaming from the Captain's Cabin and swam in there and brought out a mess attendant who had been badly injured. Another mess attendant joined me from someplace and with the water almost reaching the overhead, I emerged with the wounded mess attendant to the quarterdeck where I met Lieut. Comdr. Fuqua, USN., who gave the command, "All hands abandon ship!!", after all wounded men were put into the boats that were alongside the starboard quarterdeck. An oil fire was burning from about frame 110 forward in flames forty to fifty feet in height.

The boats were transporting the wounded men to Ford island. I dove over the stern and was later picked up well clear of the ship by a boat that was picking up survivors in the water. On orders of the senior officer, Lieut. Comdr. Fuqua, USN., I proceeded with the boat and survivors to the Landing where I stayed during the remainder of the attack.

Sgt. Jack Wilson was on duty in the Philippines when the Japanese struck:

The day the war started we had our tanks back in by the side of the runway at Clark's Field. Long about 12:30 on the first day of the war we looked up and saw a 54 airplanes and they were pretty shiny ones and we made the remark that that is a bunch of nice planes we have. Just about that time why they was over the top of us and they commenced to kicking out their bombs. They was falling every place and set the gasoline dump on fire and there was quite a bit of smoke there. Half of the boys were under a tree waiting for a chow-truck to come out. The other half, two men stayed with each tank while the other two went to eat.

Well, the chow-truck didn't come so we was underneath this tree waiting for the truck to come out. So then after the bombing raid, why the Japanese fighters came down and they commenced to shooting bullets around us and they was falling out like hail was falling and they was shooting tracers into the airplanes which was parked on the runway. Just about 30 minutes before the Japanese came, the

American planes was in the air. Then at the time the Japanese planes got there well all the men had landed and gone to the mess hall or down to the headquarters building for a meeting which they caught practically all of them on the ground except maybe one was in the air. As the bomb fell, the shrapnel cut the side of his face off and part of his shoulder. His name was Robert Brooks. They later on named the airfield at Ft. Knox after this boy because he was the first boy that was killed in the Armed Forces in WWII.

From that day, why I didn't get back to my camp bed . . . barracks . . . and I never did see my foot lockers anymore. We just kept going from one little village to another and kind of hiding out from the Japs. We didn't have too much there to fight with. Everyone was all excited and didn't know what to do. We held out for quite a bit from one town to another.

Following the surrender on Bataan, Wilson made his way to Fort Drum, a fort in Manila Bay.

I was on detail to help fire and clean the barrel of a 14-inch gun which they had there on Ft. Drum. This bullet weighed 1200 lb. and it took two bags of powder which was about the size of a sack of wheat. I imagine, about a 100 lb. sack. It took two bags of powder to fire this gun. This shell went about twenty-five miles and when this shell went off it had a detonator to it that when it went off it looked like where a bulldozer had made a pond. As we fired quite a bit of shots with that and we fought there from April 10 to may 6 which I had dinky fever quite a bit while I was there, but I kept on working and on May 6th our orders came to Ft. Drum that Corregidor had to surrender.

After the surrender the prisoners suffered terribly:

They wouldn't give us any water. We had a colonel with us there from Ft. Drum. He was from Oklahoma. He wanted to take up for the men and he'd went out there to see some of the Japanese officers was in a little cabin on up on top of the hill. So he went up there and told them the American prisoners had to have some water. And he said they 'didn't have any water for American prisoners.' And so finally there about three or four days, we'd one took all their buttons off the shirts and put them in our mouth and sucked the. Somebody had told us you'd get moisture in your mouth by sucking a button. So I don't think I had any buttons left on my shirt cause I was really trying it out anyhow.

So then from there, finally, the Japanese had told the American officer that he could have a wheelbarrow there and a 55 gallon steel drum and get some water. Well the American said, "Where's the well?" He said: "You don't get no well water," said "you get it out of the creek down here." Well this creek run into the ocean that a lot of Philippino toilets was built right over the top of this water, out over the top you know high on the bank where the toilet would be sitting. I have seen them dipping water there. They taken the thing and kind of knock the waste from the toilet away to dip the water up. And that was the only water they could get water so they filled up this barrel and brought it out there and put a lot of chlorine in it to purify the water. And it was pretty rough drinking but it was wet.

Some tried to escape:

Them boys went on and escaped that night which I didn't go with them. They was gone for about two days. They brought them back and they had tied them to fence posts, left them standing there in that hot sun without any water and kept them that way for about three days. And they wouldn't let nobody go up and talk to them, no water, no food and had their hands tied behind them and made them stoop down and put a piece of wood in-between their ankles and the upper part of their legs which this piece of wood was cutting on that piece of wood. They had their hands tied behind them on a post. So then one day they had went over and dug a big hole right in the view of all of our barracks. And they'd taken these four boys and went over and they had Japanese firing squad. And they had blind-folded these four boys and led them over there. Then they took the blindfolds off and asked them did they want a drink of water.

Some of the boys takes a little drink: some of them took a cup of water and throwed it in the Japanese face. Then they asked them did they want a cigarette. Some of them took a drink and some of the lit the cigarette and flipped it in their face because they'd been punished for three or four days without food or water and they were just two-thirds to the way dead. They had backed off these Japanese and shot them and they'd fell back in this hole and some of them squealed like a pig if you was killing hogs and didn't get a good shot on the hogs. They squealed and the Japanese run up to the hole and shot down in on them.

Saratoga were delivering supplies and equipment to the Marine garrison on Wake Island, while the U.S.S. *Enterprise* was on the west coast of the United States. It was on these three ships, and on the determination and skills of their young pilots, that the fate of the United States in the Pacific would rest in the months to come.

The U.S. was now decisively involved in World War II, and an early consequence of Pearl Harbor was the dismissal of Short and Kimmel from their commands.

The Epic Defense of Wake Island

As the attack on Pearl Harbor was unfolding, Japanese forces were moving from Kwajalein Atoll in the Marshall Islands to attack the U.S. outpost on Wake Island, where a 68-man navy and 447-man marine garrison was led by Commander Winfield Cunningham and Major James Devereux. The island was bombarded from air and sea on December 8, but the first assault by the 450-man invasion force was repulsed on December 11. Gunfire support for the Japanese was provided by three light cruisers (one modern and two old) and six destroyers. One was sunk by 5-inch coast defense artillery manned by marine gunners and another by the explosion of depth charges hit by machine-gun fire from marine Grumman F4F fighters. The Japanese then bolstered the invasion force and added two aircraft carriers (detached from the 1st Air Fleet as it returned from the Hawaiian Islands), two heavy cruisers, and two more destroyers. The new invasion force sailed on December 21, and a night assault on December 23 resulted in the defeat of the American garrison.

Guam, the southernmost of the Mariana Islands, did not fare as well as Wake Island, where a small navy and marine garrison, less than 500 men, was supported by 246 natives of the Insular Force. It was overrun on December 10 by a 5,000-man Japanese force launched from Saipan, in the Japanese part of the Marianas group, under escort of four heavy cruisers that provided devastating naval gunfire support.

Soldiers of the 7th Infantry Division take cover during the fighting for Kwajalein Atoll in the Marshall Islands, February 1944.

The capture of Wake Island provided the Japanese with an important link in their defensive perimeter, and the elimination of American strength on Guam (such as it was) helped to secure the Japanese line of communications via thr Mariana Islands. More important by far to Japanese plans, however, were the Philippine Islands. They had been U.S. possessions since the Spanish-American War of 1898, and the nature of American rule, including the promise of full independence in 1946, had made the Filipinos particularly loyal.

Strategic Importance of the Philippines

Lying some 500 miles off the coast of mainland China and dominating the eastern approaches to the China Sea, the Philippine archipelago, about 7,000 islands, has considerable strategic importance. The largest of the islands is Luzon, and in 1941 it was by far the most important in purely military terms. In 1935, General Douglas MacArthur had been appointed military adviser to the Philippine Commonwealth. MacArthur's main task, with the support of a small but highly skilled team, was to create a Filipino military establishment which would reach maturity in 1946. Implementing of MacArthur's plans was both slow and costly, however, and in 1941 the Philippine Army was wholly incapable of meeting and defeating the Japanese. The same was unfortunately true of the U.S. forces in the islands, which were not to be reinforced under the terms of the "Rainbow 5" plan and were therefore semi-expendable.

As U.S. relations with Japan soured, Filipino and American forces were combined as the United States Army Forces Far East under the command of MacArthur, who was recalled to active army service during July 1941. USAFFE had a strength of about 130,000 men, made up of 22,400 regular troops including 12,000 Philippine Scouts, 3,000 men of the

Douglas MacArthur
For further references see pages 19, 20, 21, 22, 23, 24, 27, 37, 40, 41, 42, 55, 56, 58, 60, 61, 62, 64

Philippine Constabulary, and 107,000 men of the Philippine Army, which was only partially organized, trained, and equipped. The main American formation was the Philippine Division, and while most of USAFFE's strength was deployed on Luzon, there were sizeable detachments on islands such as Cebu, Mindanao, and the Visayas. Major General Lewis H. Brereton's U.S. Far East Air Force had about 125 combat aircraft, including 35 Boeing B-17 Flying Fortress heavy bombers, with which it hoped to deter Japanese aggression. Admiral Thomas C. Hart's U.S. Asiatic Fleet had a nominal strength of three cruisers (one heavy and two light), 13 destroyers, 28 submarines, and a number of other vessels and craft, but was being withdrawn to Java in the Dutch East Indies to leave only four destroyers, the submarines, and a squadron of naval flying boats, together with one regiment of the U.S. Marine Corps in the Philippines.

MacArthur's Dispositions

The main army strength available to MacArthur was the Northern Luzon Force. Commanded by Major General Jonathan M. Wainwright and including six infantry divisions and one cavalry regiment, this unit was deployed north of Manila to meet the major Japanese assault, which MacArthur expected in Lingayen Gulf. The rest of Luzon was covered by Brigadier General George M. Parker's Southern Luzon Force, which had two divisions. Farther south still, the defense of the areas to the south was entrusted to the three divisions of Brigadier General William F. Sharp's Visayan-Mindanao Force.

The arrival of MacArthur and the B-17s injected new purpose into the defense. The basic "Orange 3" plan to yield the islands as slowly as possible was transformed. It became an offensive defense that envisaged the defeat of the invaders by counterattacks as they landed, and by B-17 attacks on their bases in Formosa. Even so, MacArthur made contingency plans for a last-ditch withdrawal into the Bataan Peninsula on the northwestern side of Manila Bay. Here in the mountainous jungles, reinforced by the complex of forts at the mouth of the bay with Corregidor as their main citadel, the defenders should be able to hold out long enough for the navy to open the way across the Pacific and allow fresh troops to arrive from the U.S.

Japan's Hasty Schedule

The Japanese had other ideas and allocated just 50,000 combat veterans of two reinforced infantry divisions as the main formations. Commanded by Lieutenant General Masaharu Homma, the Japanese 14th Army was given just 50 days to complete the conquest of the Philippines. The Japanese plan called for attacks by air units based in Formosa to paralyze the U.S. air strength. At the same time, three landings would be made, two of them in northern Luzon at Aparri and Vigan by forces from Formosa, and the third at Legaspi in southern Luzon by forces from the Palau Islands. These landings were to seize airfields from which Japanese army aircraft could destroy any American air strength that had survived the initial attacks.

These early operations would be followed by the main landings in Lingayen Gulf (43,000 men of the reinforced 48th Infantry Division from Formosa) and in Lamon Bay (a 7,000-man detachment of the 16th Infantry Division from Okinawa in the Ryukyu Islands): these two formations were to advance on Manila and then eliminate all other American and Filipino resistance on Luzon. At the same time as the Lingayen Gulf and Lamon Bay landings, a reinforced battalion from the Palaus would seize Davao in southern Mindanao as the base for operations into Borneo. Other landings would then be undertaken to secure the southern Philippines.

The men of the USAFFE were placed on alert on November 27. News of Pearl Harbor was received during the morning of December 8, and the Japanese launched minor air attacks against airfields in northern Luzon. In spite of these warnings, the Japanese achieved complete tactical surprise when 108 twin-

American air strength in the Philippines lacked both the number and the quality of aircraft that could have provided an effective resistance to the Japanese bombing effort. As a result, the Japanese had complete control of the air and could bomb whatever targets they liked. This is the scene at Cavite Navy Yard on December 13, 1941, with barges and stores blazing.

engined bombers and 34 fighters of the naval air force attacked the Clark Field and Iba airfield complex northwest of Manila at 12:15 p.m. on December 8.

Disaster at Clark Field

Most of the American aircraft were on the ground. In the resulting disaster, 18 B-17s, 56 fighters, several other aircraft, and much of the ground installations were destroyed. One American squadron was airborne; it too was virtually destroyed, though it did manage to down some of the seven Japanese fighters lost in the attack. During the following week, Japanese bombers struck at the airfields and Cavite naval base, but the surviving American bombers had been withdrawn to Mindanao on December 11 and were flown to Australia on December 17. By December 15, airworthy American fighters had been reduced to an impotent handful.

On December 10, the Tanaka and Kanno Detachments each landed 2,000 men at Aparri and Vigan; on December 12, the 2,500 men of the Kimura Detachment landed at Legaspi. The Kanno Detachment met only the lightest of opposition and divided to move north and south along Luzon's northwestern coast. The Tanaka Detachment overcame a single company at Aparri and moved up the valley of the Cagayan River to Tuguegarao, where it swept aside the rest of the battalion that had sent just a single company to Aparri. The Kimura Detachment met no significant resistance as it advanced along the Bicol Peninsula toward Manila. Japanese army aircraft were able to move into three bases on northern Luzon during December 18.

MacArthur was still sure that the main landing would be made in Lingayen Gulf and refused to allow his main strength to be drawn from this region. However, he extended the Philippine Army's 11th Division up the eastern side of Lingayen Gulf toward San Fernando, detached the Philippine Scouts' 26th Cavalry Regiment to support the 11th Division, sent one regiment of the Philippine Army's 71st Division north to intercept the Kanno and Tanaka Detachments, and shifted two companies of the Philippine Army's 51st Division west to check the Kimura Detachment.

The Japanese Land in Lingayen Gulf

These initial landings were followed in the early morning of December 22 by the main landing. MacArthur had been right: they arrived in Lingayen Gulf. However, they landed, not at the head of the gulf where the Americans and Filipinos were deployed, but on the eastern shore, where only the 71st Division was available. The landing was made on four beaches, and the Japanese encountered resistance only on the most northerly one as they moved across the sand and surged inland. The Japanese 9th Regiment drove the 71st Division back toward Baguio, and the three other invasion columns moved south along the eastern shore of the gulf to tackle the right wing of the joint forces at the head of the gulf.

With the Japanese pressing against and around the right wing of his Northern Luzon Force, Wainwright had little option. He pulled his forces back toward positions already planned. Of these, the first four were to be held lightly and used only to slow the Japanese while the fifth line was manned in strength for the decisive encounter anticipated by MacArthur and Wainwright. This movement occurred mainly as planned for the first three lines, but on the fourth line, the USAFFE formations found on December 29 that they were being outflanked.

Another Japanese Landing

Early in the morning of December 24, another Japanese invasion force had started landing in Lamon Bay against the defenses of the Southern Luzon Force. Of the two invasion forces, the more northerly was resisted strongly by the 1st Infantry Regiment of the Philippine Army's 1st Division and initially secured only a small beachhead. The southern force encountered the Philippine Army's 51st Division as it was shifting units and therefore met little resistance as it secured its beachhead and moved inland. Detaching one battalion to move into the Bicol peninsula and link up with the Kimura Detachment, the rest of the Japanese formation moved inland with the clear purpose of passing around the southern side of the Laguna de Bay and advancing on Manila.

Retreat to Bataan

MacArthur appreciated this early that the USAFFE forces would in all probability have to retreat to Bataan. On December 24, he ordered the creation of a defensive position across the northern neck of the peninsula by Parker, who passed command of the Southern Luzon Force to Major General Albert M. Jones. Parker based the defense on the Philippine Division, which was soon joined by the Philippine Army's 31st and 41st Divisions.

Manila was declared an open city and occupied by the Japanese on January 2, 1942. Meanwhile, the Southern Luzon Force was pulling back toward Bataan, and the bridges over the unfordable Pampanga River were blown up on January 1. By January 7, the surviving USAFFE forces were located in the Bataan Peninsula in two new formations, separated by the heights of Mount Natib. Considered impassable, the mountain was therefore patrolled rather than defended. On the western side was Wainwright's I Corps with the 1st, 31st, and 91st Divisions supported by the 26th Cavalry Regiment, and on the eastern side, Parker's II Corps, with the 21st, 41st, and 51st Infantry Divisions, was supported by the 57th Infantry Regiment of the Philippine Division. In addition, the 2nd and 71st Divisions of the Service Command, were available, as was a USAFFE reserve, the Philippine Division, without its 57th Infantry Regiment.

I Corps was faced by the 5,000-man Kimura Detachment, while II Corps was opposed by the 6,500-man 65th Infantry Brigade, which had by now replaced the 48th Division that was needed for operations in Java. The first phase of the fighting for the Bataan Peninsula lasted from January 7 to 26 and was characterized by several Japanese attacks that were beaten back. Yet the American and Filipino position continued to deteriorate, largely because all the supply dumps were at the end of the peninsula, and there were 20,000 refugees from Manila who had to be fed.

The Japanese Infiltrate the Defense

The decisive Japanese move took place between January 16 and 22, when part of the Japanese 9th Regiment infiltrated the patrols on Mount Natib and moved against the left flank of II Corps. This threatened to split USAFFE, and MacArthur reluctantly ordered a withdrawal from the Main Battle Position to the Reserve Battle Position farther south on the peninsula, where I and II Corps were divided by Mount Samat.

The second phase of the Bataan fighting took place between January 26 and February 8. Head-on attacks against I and II Corps were checked, even though the Kimura Detachment managed to break through I Corps' front between January 28 and February 6. On January 26, the 2nd Battalion of the Japanese 20th Regiment had secured amphibious beachheads on the western side of the peninsula at Quinauan and Longoskayan Points, and a third beachhead had been established on January 26 on Canas Point by the 1st Battalion of the same regiment. These beachheads were eliminated on February 8, January 29, and February 13 respectively by a combination of direct attack, long-range artillery bombardment, and

The U.S. Navy's most important fighter of World War II was the Grumman F6F Hellcat. It was clearly derived from the same company's F4F, which had been the best U.S. carrierborne fighter at the beginning of the war, but was larger, had a considerably more powerful engine for higher performance, and carried heavier armament. The Hellcat could also double in the fighter-bomber role.

harassment by PT boats. On February 8, Homma pulled his forces back from the main front and decided to await reinforcement before resuming the offensive.

MacArthur Leaves the Philippines

On March 11, President Roosevelt ordered MacArthur to leave the Philippines, and the general arrived in Australia on March 17 to assume command of the Allied forces of the Southwest Pacific Area. Before his departure, MacArthur divided his forces into the Mindanao, Visayan, Harbor Defenses, and Luzon Forces, responsible to him via a forward headquarters on Corregidor, and Wainwright assumed command of the Luzon Force, with Major General Jones taking over I Corps. In Washington, General George C. Marshall, the U.S. Army Chief of Staff, knew nothing of MacArthur's arrangement and appointed Lieutenant General Wainwright commander of what were now the U.S. Forces in the Philippines. There was considerable confusion until Wainwright was confirmed in this position on March 20, and Major General Edward P. King took over the Luzon Force. American morale was still high, especially as a number of Japanese attacks had been driven back, but the performance of the troops was declining steadily as a result of malnutrition and disease. Rations had been halved on January 7, and they were halved again during March. Disease was already a problem, and the weakening caused by lack of food became so great a factor that, by the end of March, some 24,000 Americans were hospitalized or convalescing.

These Douglas SBD Dauntless dive-bombers of VS-6 (Scout Squadron Six) are flying over the fleet carrier *Enterprise* and an escorting destroyer.

Franklin D. Roosevelt
For further references see pages 105, *131*

War of Attrition

During this period, the Japanese 14th Army kept up a war of attrition. It was also reinforced with the 4th and 21st Divisions. On April 3, a heavy air and artillery bombardment that had started in mid-March climaxed in a furious storm that paved the way for the decisive Japanese assault. Pinning attacks were launched against I Corps on the American left, but the main Japanese weight was concentrated against the American right. The 41st Division crumbled in the face of three assault columns, and the Japanese advanced ten miles in 48 hours. I Corps tried to take the Japanese breakthrough formations in flank, but was repulsed without difficulty while II Corps disintegrated as a fighting formation.

Surrender on Bataan

The result was now a foregone conclusion, and on March 9, King agreed to the unconditional surrender of the Luzon Force. The Japanese allowed most of the Filipinos to return home, but American and Filipino regulars were herded off on the infamous "Bataan death march" along the 90 miles to Camp O'Donnell. Many died, swelling the already considerable total of about 20,000 men who had become casualties during the Bataan campaign.

Homma was furious that the surrender had not included all American and Filipino forces in the Philippines and now turned his attention to Corregidor. Together with its satellite forts in the mouth of Manila Bay, MacArthur's stronghold had been under sporadic air and artillery bombardment since early in February. This bombardment intensified to a crescendo between April 10 and May 6. With the exception of the 14-inch turret guns on Fort Drum, all the American artillery positions were open-topped. They suffered terribly as the Japanese added a barrage of artillery fire from Bataan and Cavite to their bombing attacks. Virtually everything on Corregidor except the command and hospital tunnel inside Malinta Hill was destroyed, and the defenders were both shell-shocked and virtually out of water when the 1st Battalion of the Japanese 61st Regiment landed near Cavalry Point on the island's northern shore on May 5. Another battalion soon followed, and there was nothing that the Americans could do to halt the invaders. Wainwright started surrender negotiations on May 6, and the Japanese cancelled their plan for another landing, at James Ravine, during the following night.

The End in the Philippines

Homma demanded that Wainwright surrender all the remaining American and Filipino forces in the Philippines, and on May 10 and 11 Brigadier General Sharp and Brigadier General Bradford G. Chynoweth surrendered their Mindanao and Visayan Forces. These comparatively small forces had been fighting the penetrations of the southern Philippine Islands after a series of Japanese landings on Jolo, Mindanao, Cebu, and Panay islands. At the same time, they had been laying the foundations for a guerrilla organization which became a serious thorn in the side of the Japanese occupation in the years to come.

By this time, the Japanese had completed their conquest of Malaya and the East Indies, and were deep into Burma. Japan wanted Malaya and Burma for a variety of reasons, but the core of the Southern Resources Area was the East Indies. The islands offered oil, rubber, and other strategically important raw materials; they were the treasure house of the Greater East Asia Co-Prosperity Sphere.

The Japanese Advance into the East Indies

The East Indies are made up of a vast number of islands. Defense was difficult for a variety of reasons, including a shortage of roads on even the larger islands. The Dutch based their defensive scheme on air power operating from a large number of airfields, but by the time the Japanese turned their attentions to

Edward P. King
For further references
see pages
23, 28, *37*, 40

Though many pre-war naval strategists thought that the battleship would be the arbiter of any naval war in the Pacific, events proved them wrong. The aircraft carrier emerged as the decisive naval weapon, though the battleship remained vitally important for defending carriers and bombarding of shore targets. This photograph shows 16-in projectiles moving from a battleship's stationary shell platform to the rotating section that formed one of the ship's turrets. This section turned as the turret traversed, and shells could then be hoisted into position behind the gun breeches.

the East Indies, the Allies had precious few warplanes with which to bolster the inadequate number of Dutch aircraft in the islands. The Dutch ground forces were largely made up of local troops trained and equipped for internal security duties, and Allied naval power was based on a miscellany of obsolescent Dutch ships supported by American, Australian, and British warships.

By the time the Japanese moved on the East Indies, defense had been entrusted to ABDACOM (American-British-Dutch-Australian Command) headed by a British general with an American officer, Admiral Hart, as his naval commander. The course of operations was complex in terms of timings and movements, but was basically simple in tactics. The series of Japanese invasions in January and February 1941 used three naval task forces, with troops supplied by the Japanese 16th Army.

The primary objectives were any ports which had an airfield nearby. The Japanese used land-based aircraft to destroy Allied air capability on the airfield and then landed army or navy troops under cover of air power from carriers. With Allied ground forces neutralized, the airfield was then restored to operational capability, Japanese land-based aircraft moved in, and the Japanese advance through the East Indies leapfrogged forward. All this time, the main Allied naval bases were kept under air bombardment to prevent Allied ships from intercepting invasion forces. All their attempts at air reconnaissance were destroyed, so the Allies were forced to work in the dark about Japanese movements and intentions.

American Naval Involvement

Four American destroyers intercepted a Japanese convoy off Balikpapan on January 23/24, 1942. In the Battle of Macassar Strait, they sank five Japanese ships (one light warship and four troop transports), but did nothing to slow the pace of the Japanese tide. The next engagement of the period that involved American warships was the Battle of Madoera Strait on February 4. Japanese bombers struck a combined American and Dutch squadron. They severely damaged the heavy cruiser U.S.S. *Houston* and the light cruiser U.S.S. *Marblehead*, which had to limp away to the United States for repairs, leaving the *Houston* as the only major American warship in the area.

On February 12/13, an American, British, and Dutch squadron tried to intercept a Japanese convoy preparing to land troops on Sumatra, but in the Battle off Palembang was driven back by Japanese bombers. On February 14, Hart was succeeded as ABDACOM naval commander by a Dutch officer. Further naval activity followed before the decisive Battle of the Java Sea on February 27. A Dutch-commanded squadron of five cruisers and ten destroyers tried to intercept a Japanese invasion force making for eastern Java. The Japanese force included four cruisers and 13 destroyers, and in a seven-hour running battle, the Allied squadron was crushed. The *Houston* and four U.S. destroyers were among the survivors.

ABDACOM had been dissolved on February 25, and as they attempted to reach Australia several American, Australian, and British ships ran into a Japanese force on February 28. In the Battle off Banten Bay, most of the Allied ships were sunk, and the only U.S. ships to reach Australia were four destroyers. On March 9, the Dutch surrendered the East Indies to the Japanese. The Japanese had not only secured the core of the Southern Resources area; they had also driven a strategically important wedge

between the British-led forces in the Indian Ocean and American-led forces in the Pacific.

American Strategic Reorganization

This factor led to a reorganization, completed on March 30, 1942, of the Allied command structure for the war against Japan. Britain would direct strategy in the area west of the Japanese wedge (India, Burma, Malaya, and Sumatra). East of the wedge, the United States would organize and direct strategy. MacArthur commanded the Southwest Pacific Area, and Admiral Chester W. Nimitz took charge of the three-section Pacific Ocean Areas.

An essential component in this reorganization was the finalization of a major supply route from the United States to Australia, which was the bastion from which MacArthur's forces were to return toward the Philippines. This supply line ran from west coast ports such as Seattle, San Francisco, and Los Angeles southwest to the Hawaiian Islands and then in a great loop to Brisbane in eastern Australia. Hawaii was strongly reinforced, and air, naval, and logistical bases were established and garrisoned on islands close to the route such as Palmyra, Canton, Samoa, Fiji, and New Caledonia.

Over the same period, other Japanese forces were striking southeast into areas governed by Australia, using the same basic tactics that they had employed in the East Indies. On January 23, the Japanese 4th Fleet coordinated the capture of Kavieng on New Ireland and Rabaul on New Britain as the main bases for further operations in this area. After an early consolidation, the Japanese moved forward during March 1942 to Lae and Salamaua in New Guinea, and to Buka and Bougainville islands in the Solomon Islands.

CV-10 was the second fleet aircraft carrier *Yorktown*, named for the first ship, CV-5, which was lost on June 7, 1942. CV-10 was the second unit of the ten-strong group of the 26 "Essex" class vessels that formed the backbone of the Pacific fleet's carrier strength in the second half of World War II. The class was based on the three-strong "Yorktown" class, but had larger hulls, greater displacement, and a host of improved features, including an outboard elevator and a flight deck that overhung the hull on the port side. The ships displaced 27,100 tons. The first group had an overall length of 872 feet, while the second group had a comparable length of 888 feet. The ships each carried a defensive armament of twelve 5-in guns (in four twin turrets and four single mountings), and between forty-four and sixty- eight 40-mm Bofors guns, and could carry up to 100 aircraft. Power was provided by four sets of geared steam turbines delivering 150,000 hp to four shafts, which generated a speed of 33 knots.

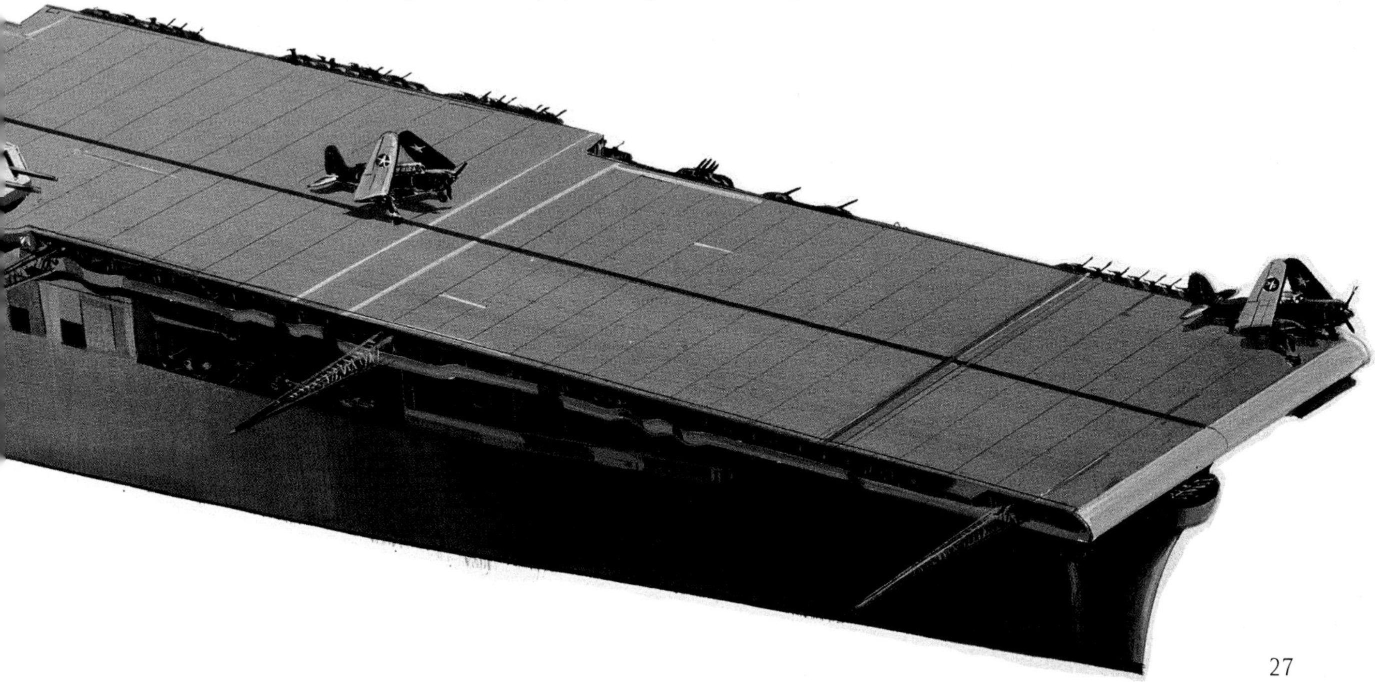

Admiral Chester W. Nimitz, who headed the Pacific Ocean Areas through most of World War II, was also commander-in-chief of the Pacific Fleet. His contribution to victory over the Japanese was enormous.

The Navy Takes the Offensive

The Allies were certainly on the strategic defensive, but the U.S. Navy was determined to take the offensive wherever possible. The weapon for this task was the Pacific Fleet's aircraft carriers, which had escaped the debacle at Pearl Harbor. In January 1942, Admiral Ernest J. King, the new Chief of Naval Operations, ordered Nimitz's Pacific Ocean Areas command to take the offensive as soon as possible. The object was to harass the Japanese in forward areas as the fleet's strength was rebuilt in the Hawaiian Islands and on the west coast. Nimitz's task was complicated by severe damage inflicted on the *Saratoga* by a torpedo from a Japanese submarine on January 11, but the arrival of the U.S.S. *Yorktown* from the Atlantic Fleet soon after restored the Pacific Fleet's carrier strength.

On February 1, Vice Admiral William F. Halsey led the *Enterprise* and *Yorktown*, with an escort of cruisers and destroyers, on a raid against the Japanese bases in the Gilbert and Marshall islands. Some damage was done to the Japanese installations, and the raiding force returned safely to Pearl Harbor. Later in the month, Vice Admiral Wilson Brown's task force, centered on the *Lexington* moved through the Solomon Sea to attack the Japanese base at Rabaul. The task force was detected by Japanese aircraft on February 20 and brought under air attack. The Americans broke off their attempt to pound Rabaul, but inflicted severe losses on the Japanese aircraft that tried to sink the *Lexington*. Halsey's *Enterprise* task force moved out again later in February, attacking Wake Island on February 24 and Marcus Island on March 4 before returning to Pearl Harbor. The *Lexington* was meanwhile joined by the *Yorktown*, and under Brown's command the two carriers cruised in the Coral Sea. Carrier-based aircraft flew across the Owen Stanley Mountains in New Guinea for an attack on Lae and Salamaua on March 10, in which several Japanese light warships and transports were damaged and sunk.

Chester Nimitz
For further references see pages 27, 29, 32, 37, 40, 58, 73, 74, 76, 90, 93, 105, 107, 117

The "Doolittle Raid"

An enormous pshychological boost during this period came from the "Doolittle raid" against Tokyo. Commanded by Lieutenant Colonel James H. Doolittle, 16 North American B-25 Mitchell medium bombers of the Army Air Forces were launched from the carrier U.S.S. *Hornet* on April 18 for the perilous 800-mile flight to Japan. With the exception of one bomber that landed in Siberia and was interned with its crew, the aircraft were lost or forced to crash-land in China. Despite the negligible amount of damage caused to the Japanese capital, the raid greatly boosted U.S. morale. It was also instrumental in persuading the Japanese to extend their defensive perimeter to try to prevent any repetition of the raid.

As the first steps in this Japanese expansion, the Japanese decided to seize seaplane bases in the Louisiade Islands and in the southeastern part of the Solomon Islands, and also to capture Port Moresby. Located on the southern side of eastern New Guinea, Port Moresby was the main Allied base on the island. To establish the base in the southeastern Solomons at Tulagi on Florida Island, the Japanese 4th Fleet despatched the small carrier *Shoho*, four cruisers, and one destroyer to escort the troop transports. At the same time, a larger amphibious force was being assembled at Rabaul for the operation against Port Moresby. Additional air support was needed there, so the carriers *Shokaku* and *Zuikaku*, veterans of the Pearl Harbor attack, were sent south through the central Pacific to enter the Coral Sea from the east.

The United States was able to decipher the Japanese naval code, so the Americans knew what was developing. Nimitz sent Rear Admiral Frank J. Fletcher's Task Force 17, based on the carrier *Yorktown*, to intercept the Japanese. On May 3, the Japanese landed on Florida Island. There was no opposition, so the *Shoho* sailed to join the Port Moresby operation. The Yorktown was meanwhile sailing north. On May 4, Fletcher launched part of the carrier's air strength to attack the

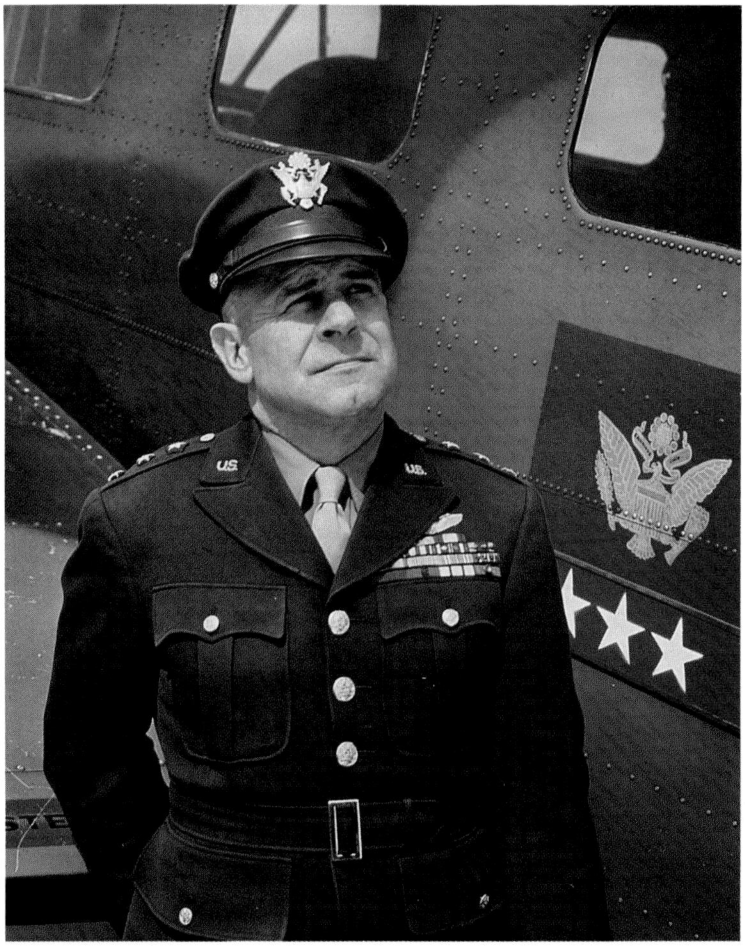

Above: Pictured here in the rank of lieutenant general, James H. Doolittle was a famed pre-war pilot whose first real contribution to the American effort in World War II was the "Doolittle raid" flown against Tokyo in April 1942 by army bombers launched from a navy aircraft carrier

Left: An epic moment: a North American B-25 Mitchell medium bomber of the U.S. Army Air Forces leaves the flight deck of the fleet carrier *Hornet* on April 18, 1942, for the "Doolittle raid" on Tokyo.

Captain Marc A. Mitscher of the *Hornet* chats with Lieutenant Colonel Doolittle and men of his detachment before the "Doolittle raid." Both Mitscher and Doolittle were destined for greater things – and senior command – as the war progressed.

Japanese on Florida Island. After recovering the aircraft, Fletcher swung south again into the Coral Sea. There, he was joined on May 6 by Rear Admiral Aubrey W. Fitch's Task Force 11 (centered on the carrier *Lexington*) and the British-commanded Task Force 44 of American and Australian cruisers with escorting destroyers.

The Battle of the Coral Sea

The result was the Battle of the Coral Sea on May 7/8. This encounter was the first example of a new type of naval action. The protagonists never came within sight of each other, they fought the battle with carrier-based aircraft. The *Shoho* was sunk by American aircraft on May 7, and an attempted Japanese night attack on May 7/8 resulted only in the loss of many Japanese aircraft. The following morning, however, an exchange of raids resulted in the sinking of the *Lexington* and some damage to the *Yorktown*. The *Shokaku* was severely damaged, but the *Zuikaku* escaped any damage. The U.S. lost a destroyer and a fleet oiler before the battle ended.

The Battle of the Coral Sea might have been a tactical defeat for the Allies, as they had lost one large carrier while sinking only one small carrier. The Japanese had lost a larger number of aircraft than the Allies, together with their invaluable aircrew. Strategically, however, the battle was an Allied victory; the Japanese called off their amphibious invasion of Port Moresby and the Louisiade Islands. The Japanese navy was relieved of its task, and on July 22 a reinforced engineer regiment landed at Gona on the northeast coast of New Guinea to prepare for an overland attack on Port Moresby.

Yamamoto's Ambitious Plan

Another result of the "Doolittle raid" and Japan's decision to expand her defensive perimeter was the Battle of Midway. This action, planned by Yamamoto, had two objectives: to secure Midway Island as the eastern linchpin of a widened Japanese

Isoroku Yamamoto
For further references see pages 10, 31, 32, 34, 35, 50, *53*, 56, 65, 93

Above: The U.S. Navy's most important carrierborne torpedo bomber of World War II was the Grumman TBF Avenger. The type replaced the obsolete Douglas TBD Devastator from mid-1942 and played a major part in the eventual American triumph. These Avengers, seen during weapon-release practice, were based at the Naval Air Station in Norfolk, Virginia.

Left: The Japanese light carrier *Shoho* burns after being torpedoed in the Battle of the Coral Sea on May 7, 1942. The ship later sank, the first Japanese carrier lost in World War II.

perimeter in the central Pacific, and to lure the remnants of the Pacific Fleet into a battle that would result in the complete annihilation of American naval power in the Pacific. Yamamoto believed that the *Yorktown* and *Lexington* had both been sunk in the Battle of the Coral Sea, and he had information that the *Enterprise* and *Hornet* were both still in the South Pacific.

Although he felt that his Midway operation would not be opposed by any Allied carriers, Yamamoto nonetheless concentrated no fewer than 165 ships to crack this apparently weak nut.

An explosion rips through the fleet carrier *Lexington* during the Battle of the Coral Sea, almost casually tossing a plane over the side. The ship sank on May 8, 1942.

The rest of the Combined Fleet was allocated to the Midway operation, divided into three main forces: Nagumo's 1st Carrier Strike Force, Vice-Admiral Nobutake Kondo's Support Force (2nd Fleet), and Yamamoto's own Main Force (1st Fleet). The 1st Carrier Strike Force numbered four carriers, two battleships, two heavy cruisers, one light cruiser, 12 destroyers, and eight tankers. The Support Force included one light carrier, two battleships, four heavy cruisers, one light cruiser, eight destroyers, and four tankers. The Main Force had one light carrier, three battleships (including the super-battleship *Yamato* with nine 18·1-inch guns), one light cruiser, and nine destroyers.

Sailing from the Japanese base at Kure, the Support Force was to rendezvous with Midway Occupation Force, a two-part body moving from the Mariana Islands as Rear Admiral Raizo Tanaka's Occupation Force (one light cruiser, ten destroyers, one tanker, and 15 transports with 5,000 troops) and Rear Admiral Takeo Kurita's Occupation Support Force (four heavy cruisers, three destroyers, and two seaplane tenders). These forces were to move on Midway Island from the southwest, draw Allied naval forces into the arena selected by Yamamoto, and seize the island.

Moving from Kure, the 1st Carrier Strike Force and Main Force were to reach a point northwest of Midway and then fall on the Allied naval strength drawn forward by the Midway forces. To provide advance warning of American movements, and to attack any suitable targets of opportunity, Yamamoto placed a cordon of 18 submarines in an arc running between west and northwest of the Hawaiian Islands.

The Navy in the Know

Warned by naval intelligence of the unfolding Japanese plan, Nimitz recalled the *Enterprise* and *Hornet* from the South Pacific, and dockyard workers repaired the *Yorktown* in just 48 hours instead of the estimated three months. Thus, Nimitz would have three carriers and about 250 warplanes, about the same number as Nagumo's four Pearl Harbor veteran carriers. With a total of 76 warships at his disposal, Nimitz detached about one-third to Alaskan waters as Rear Admiral Robert A. Theobald's Task Force 8, whose main strength lay in two heavy cruisers, three light cruisers, 13 destroyers and six submarines.

Using his knowledge of Yamamoto's basic strength, plans, and dispositions, Nimitz decided to fight the battle within air range of Midway Island, which would bolster U.S. air strength by the 109 land-based army, navy, and marine aircraft on the island. By late May, Nimitz had grouped his major forces north of Midway Island without being detected by the Japanese submarine cordon, and thereby gained the all-important tactical initiative. Nimitz remained in Pearl Harbor and gave tactical command to Fletcher as Halsey was ill. Fletcher had his own TF17 and Rear Admiral Raymond A. Spruance's TF16. TF17 had one carrier (the *Yorktown*), two heavy cruisers, and six destroyers, while TF16 included two carriers (the *Enterprise* and *Hornet*), five heavy cruisers, one light cruiser, and 11 destroyers. A cordon of 12 U.S. submarines ran in an arc from northwest to

Raymond A. Spruance

For further references see pages 33, 35, 43, 47, 50

southwest around Midway; a wider arc was patrolled by land-based aircraft from June 3.

Operations in the Aleutians

Outmaneuvring TF8, the Japanese Northern Area Force proceeded with its part of the operation without any real interference. Aircraft from Rear Admiral Kakuji Kakuta's 2nd Carrier Strike Force (two light carriers, two heavy cruisers, four destroyers, and one seaplane tender) attacked Dutch Harbor, on the central Aleutian island of Umnak, on June 3 and 4. Japanese soldiers from the two occupation forces then seized Kiska and Attu, at the western end of the island chain, during June 6 and 7 respectively. The Allies knew this was only a diversion and made no real effort to halt the operation, even though it left two pieces of U.S. territory in Japanese hands.

The Battle of Midway Starts with Japanese Success

The first phase of the Battle of Midway began at 3:00 a.m. on June 4. Thinking that there were no American carriers in the area, Nagumo launched about half of his aircraft (108 warplanes) against Midway. At the same time, Midway launched most of its aircraft to attack the incoming bombers and strike at the Japanese carriers. This phase lasted until 7:00 a.m. and resulted in a Japanese success. The obsolete Allied aircraft suffered heavy losses, while inflicting no real damage on the Japanese aircraft or carriers. The Japanese aircraft, on the other hand, broke through to Midway and caused considerable damage.

The second phase of the battle began at 7:00 a.m. after Nagumo had received word from his first attack wave that more bombing was needed on the island. Nagumo ordered the use of fragmentation and incendiary bombs instead of the armor-piercing bombs and torpedoes carried by the attack planes still on his carriers. It took about an hour to make the switch. While the job was well underway, aerial reconnaissance revealed to a startled Nagumo that there was a large body of American warships to the northeast. The Japanese admiral changed his mind once more and ordered the newly installed land-attack weapons to be replaced once more by ship-attack weapons. More delays resulted as the Midway attack aircraft were being recovered, and Nagumo later shifted course from southeast to northeast in an effort to get close to the reported American concentration.

Seen here in the rank of vice admiral, Raymond A. Spruance was a commander who rose mangificently to the challenge of commanding major naval formations in the particular operational and tactical conditions that developed in the Pacific Ocean.

The Allies Score a Stunning Success

The Japanese force had been detected by Allied reconnaissance at 5:34 a.m. At 7:00 a.m., Fletcher ordered Spruance to launch the aircraft from the *Enterprise* and the *Hornet*, which departed from 7:52 a.m. *Yorktown* launched half her aircraft just over an hour later. Spruance's dive bombers missed the

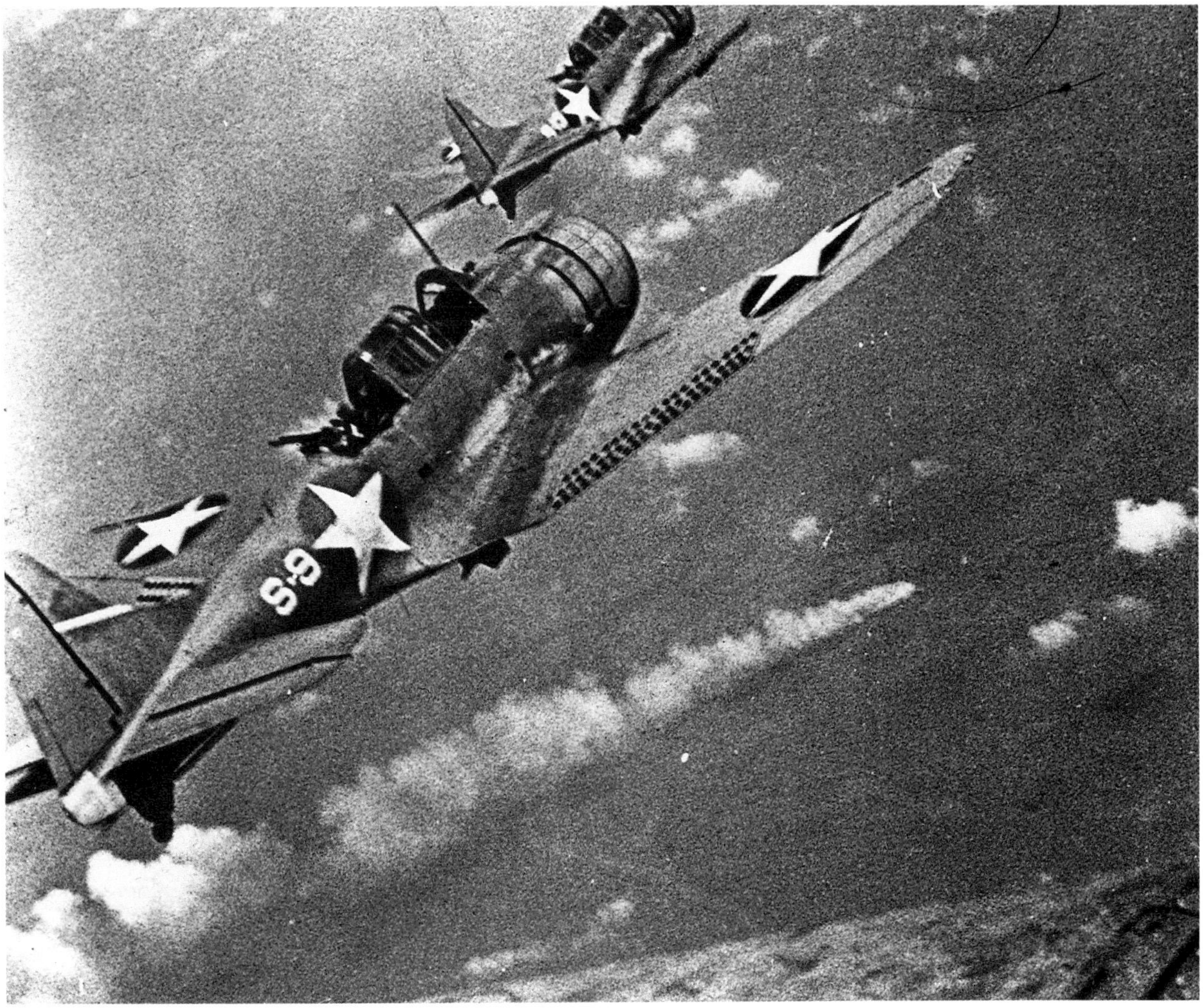

Despite its blurred quality, this remains a classic photograph of Douglas SBD Dauntless dive-bombers in action during the Battle of Midway. Below the aircraft is the plume of smoke from a burning Japanese ship. The fact that the Dauntlesses are on their way to an attack is confirmed by the bombs just visible under the fuselages of the two machines.

Japanese carriers after Nagumo's change of course, but the Douglas TBD Devastator torpedo bombers spotted their targets and bored in, straight and level without any escort by Grumman F4F Wildcat fighters. The result was inevitable, and the combination of Japanese fighters and antiaircraft gunners ripped them to pieces. Nagumo thought that he had destroyed all Allied aircraft in the area and continued re-arming his own aircraft. At last, the Douglas SBD Dauntless dive bombers found the Japanese carriers in their box formation, their decks covered by aircraft being rearmed and refueled. The squadrons from the *Enterprise*, *Hornet*, and *Yorktown* attacked in that order, and by 10:35 a.m. the *Akagi*, *Kaga*, and *Soryu* were flaming wrecks.

However, the fourth Japanese carrier, *Hiryu*, was still completely operational and at 11:00 a.m. launched her strike aircraft. They found the *Yorktown* and hit her with three bombs between 12:05 and 12:15 p.m. Other Japanese aircraft arrived in due course and at 2:30 p.m. scored two major torpedo hits. At 3:00 p.m., Fletcher ordered the Yorktown to be abandoned.

Two hours later, 24 Dauntlesses from the *Enterprise* attacked the *Hiryu*, scored several hits, and set this last Japanese carrier on fire. The Japanese abandoned the ship at 5:10 a.m. on June 5, and she sank at 9:00 a.m.

A Total Disaster for the Japanese

Yamamoto had already paid an enormous price for the tactical error of separating the 1st Carrier Strike Force and Main Body beyond mutual support distance. He was dumbfounded by the

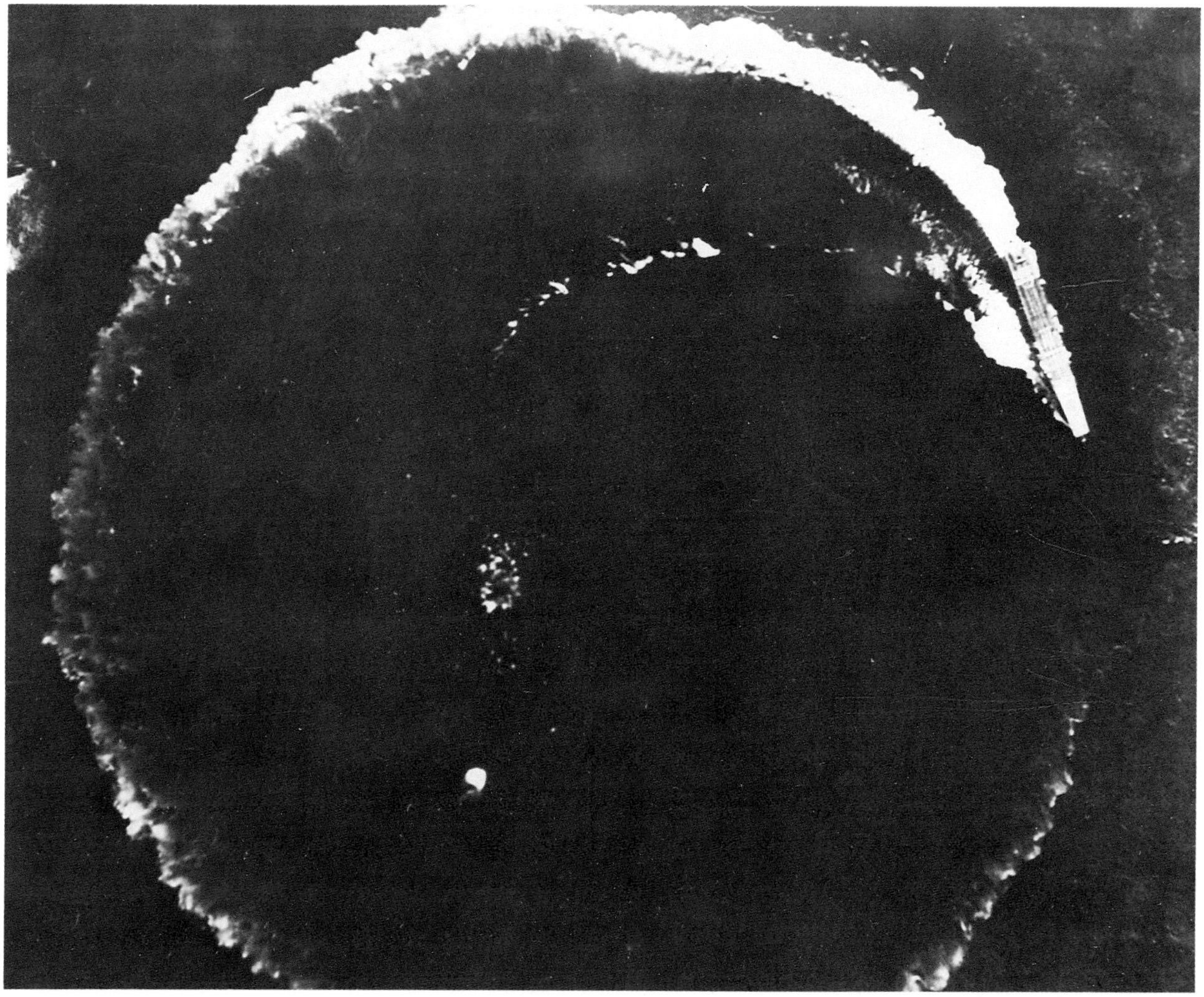

Photographed from a Boeing B-17 Flying Fortress bomber of the U.S. Army Air Forces, this Japanese carrier is circling in an effort to avoid American bombs during the Battle of Midway. Despite their best efforts, the Japanese still lost four of their invaluable fleet carriers in the battle.

news of the complete loss of the 1st Carrier Strike Force's main ships. Even so, he was determined to have some success, and during the night of June 4/5, the third phase of the battle unfolded. Yamamoto headed east at top speed in the hope of getting the U.S. carriers within range of his battleships' guns. But Spruance, to whom Fletcher had given command after the *Yorktown*'s loss, was too wily to fall for such a move and had already turned his forces away. Soon after midnight, Yamamoto realized that his plan had failed. Lacking the air cover that was now so obviously vital, he reversed course to the west and called off the invasion of Midway Island.

The last phase of the battle took place during June 5 and 6. The Americans pursued the Japanese by day, but hung back by night in case Yamamoto tried to spring another trap on them. The Japanese suffered additional damage, but Spruance finally turned back toward Pearl Harbor as his ships were running short of fuel.

Loss of the *Yorktown*

The *Yorktown* was meanwhile being towed back toward Pearl Harbor. The disabled carrier was spotted and sunk, together with an escorting destroyer, by a Japanese submarine. They were the only American ship losses of the Battle of Midway, which also cost the Allies 132 land-and carrier-based aircraft, as well as 307 men killed.

Japanese losses were the four carriers, one heavy cruiser, and 275 aircraft, as well as 3,600 men killed. More important, defeat in the Battle of Midway deprived Japan of her long-range naval

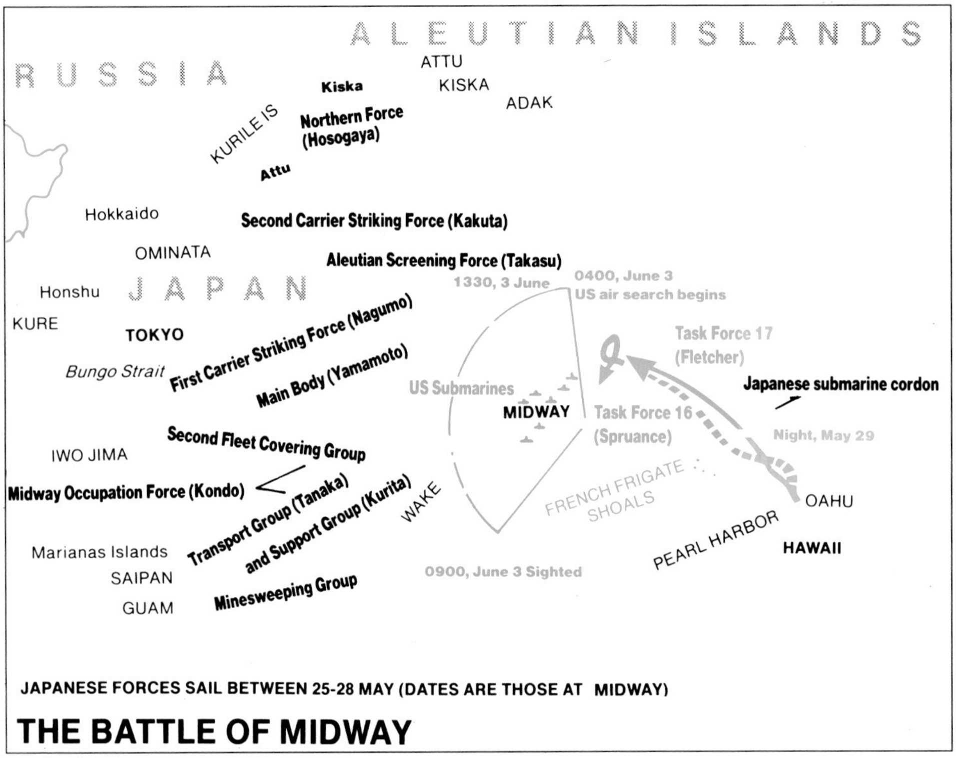

The Battle of Midway was planned by Admiral Yamamoto as a typically complex operation, but resulted in the decisive defeat of the Japanese aircraft carrier arm.

strike power. The ships and aircraft could be replaced, even if slowly, but nothing could be done to match this materiel with crews who had the combat experience and skill of those who had been lost in the Battles of the Coral Sea and Midway.

One of History's Most Decisive Battles

The Battle of Midway turned the tide of the war against Japan, and so it took its place as one of the most decisive and important battles in history. At a single stroke, the Battle of Midway halted the flood of Japanese expansion. Japan's conquests were admittedly large, but their very extent helped to conceal the fact that Japan's new empire was poorly conceived from a military point of view. The length of the empire's perimeter made it difficult to protect, and Japan was now faced with the problem of a sustained war against an enemy who was industrially superior and becoming technically more advanced. Japan had gambled everything on a short war, and her war-making capability (armed forces, associated industries, and fuel supplies) was wholly inadequate even to sustain the current effort, let alone withstand the strength that the United States was beginning to develop and deploy. Japan's merchant shipping fleet was just large enough to ferry men and supplies out to the defensive perimeter and to bring back raw materials from the Southern Resources Area. As soon as the U.S. submarine fleet began its devastating campaign against the Japanese merchant fleet, even these tasks were beyond it.

Even so, the Japanese felt that they could continue their offensive effort in one area and still gain useful strategic results. This region was eastern New Guinea and the island groups lying to its north and east, the Bismarck archipelago and the Solomon Islands. Japan had planned to push forward as far as New Caledonia, Fiji, and Samoa. Their objective was to cut the maritime supply route linking the United States and Australia, which would force the U.S. to use a longer, less efficient route deeper through the South Pacific. Such an offensive was clearly no longer a practical proposition, but the Japanese realized that it was essential to capture Port Moresby and the eastern end of the Solomon Islands. From these bases, they could check any Allied counteroffensive and provide positions from which Japanese bombers could attack the Allied supply route. The two major results of this Japanese decision were an overland advance toward Port Moresby, and the establishment of an air base on the island of Guadalcanal.

Allied Buildup

During this period, there had been a considerable buildup of Allied forces in the region. The Australian forces serving in the Middle East were recalled, and both Australia and New Zealand raised additional formations. At the same time, American men and equipment arrived in an ever-increasing stream. Despite the "Germany first" policy, four times as many American fighting men were sent to the Pacific as to Europe during the early part of 1942. This diversion of men involved an even heavier diversion of shipping, for the delivery of a U.S. division to Australia took twice the tonnage of a division moved to Europe.

Behind the steady acceleration of U.S. forces delivered into the Pacific was Admiral King, who, with most other naval officers, had come to regard the Pacific as the navy's own particular backyard. The navy wanted to make the war with Japan its first priority. To do this, it needed the army to deliver large numbers of men and vast quantities of equipment to the Pacific urgently. The army was willing to send enough men and equipment to stem the Japanese advance, but the navy argued that the best way to prevent any further Japanese offensive plans was to launch aggressive operations. These actions would keep the Japanese off balance and ease the Allied task of building up forces for the decisive counteroffensives.

Differing Army and Navy Plans

These differences of opinion between army and navy commanders confused the development of operations against the Japanese. The problems were compounded by the military philosophies of the two major commanders in the area. MacArthur, emotionally tied to the concept of liberating the Philippines, saw his base in Australia as the ideal launching pad for the army to move northwest through the eastern East Indies to the Philippines. Nimitz was a firm believer in navy-dominated operations directed from Hawaii Islands west through the island groups of the central Pacific toward Japan. Both MacArthur and Nimitz saw his own command area as the decisive one, and each tried to get priority in men and equipment.

After the Battle of Midway, the navy clearly had the advantage over its Japanese rival. However, it lay in the Pacific Fleet's aircraft carriers. The loss of even one of these ships would jeopardize the advantage. It was clear that the time was not yet ripe for the navy to drive through the central Pacific, so planners in both services looked for an area where their limited forces could be deployed in an operation that would wreak maximum

Admiral Ernest J. King was the professional head of the U.S. Navy through most of World War II. From his office in Washington, he exercised strong administrative control over the ever-strengthening force of U.S. submarines, surface ships, and aircraft. Like most naval officers, King keenly advocated the use of a greater proportion of American resources in the war against Japan.

The Japanese battleship *Kirishima*, the third of the four-strong "Kongo" class, was sunk on November 15, 1942. The class, designed in the United Kingdom by Sir George Thurston, embodied the lessons learned in the design of the British "Lion" class of battlecruisers. The lead ship was built in a British yard, and the other three were produced in Japanese yards. They were launched as pairs in 1912 and 1913. The ships were completed as battlecruisers, but after extensive reconstruction in 1930 and 1936, they were reclassified as battleships. The *Kirishima* displaced 31,980 tons, had an overall length of 729 ft 6 in, and her four seats of steam turbines delivered 136,000 hp to four propeller shafts for a maximum speed of 30·5 knots. The main battery had eight 14-in guns in four twin turrets, the secondary battery included fourteen 6-in guns in single turrets, and the antiaircraft battery totaled eight 5-in guns in four twin turrets and twenty 25-mm cannon in two twin mountings. The two units that survived Guadalcanal received steadily upgraded antiaircraft defense that eventually reached between ninety-four and one hundred and eighteen 25-mm cannon, even though the number of 5-in guns was reduced to 12.

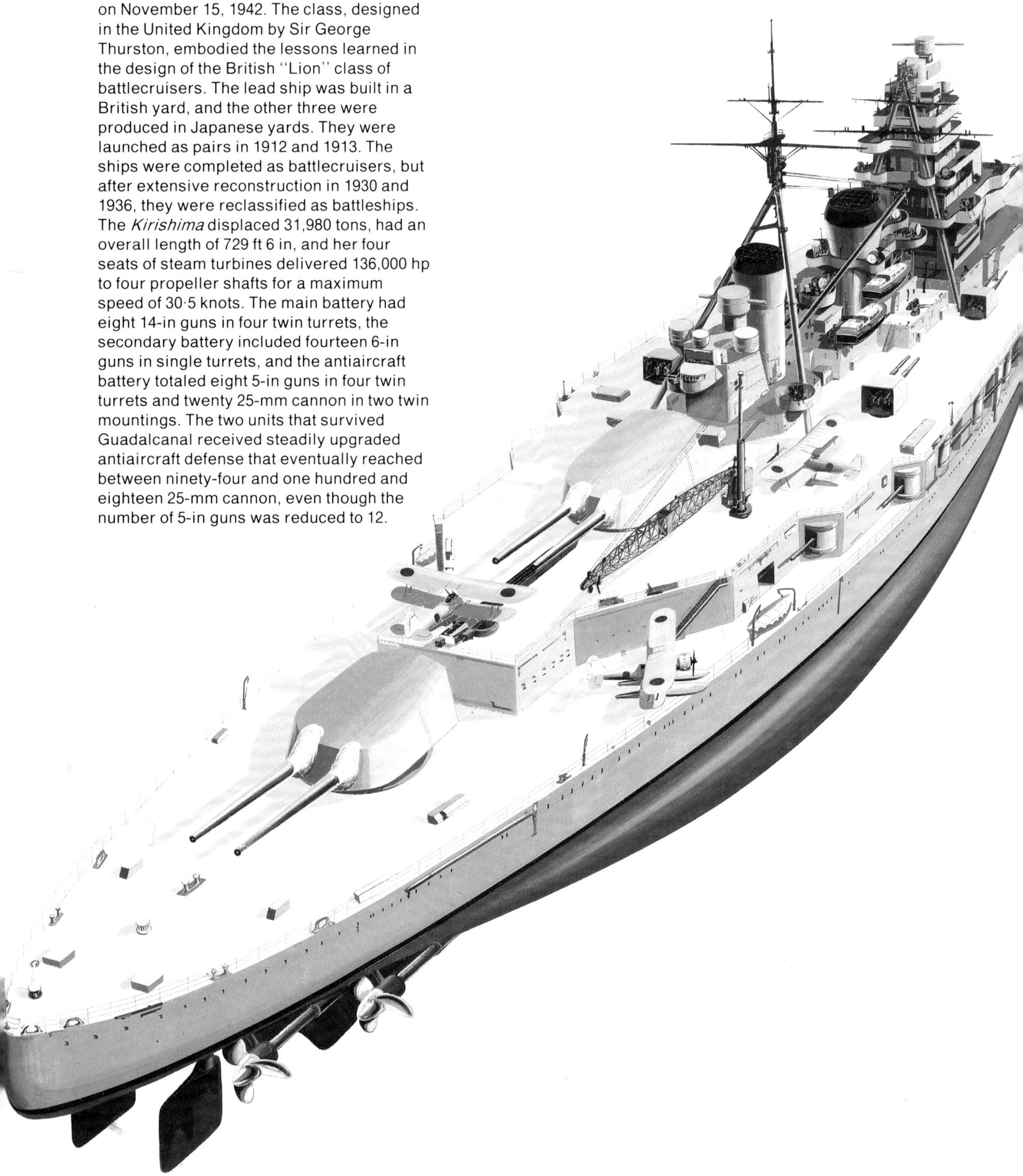

The high point of American battleship design and construction in World War II was the four units of the "Iowa" class. These ships were about 200 feet longer than the four units of the preceeding "South Dakota" class. They had a displacement about 10,000 tons greater, but carried the same primary and secondary batteries. The superiority of the "Iowa" design lay in its considerably superior protection, and the weight of this protection demanded a longer hull. Its high length-to-breadth ratio combined with its huge power to provide a maximum speed of 33 knots, the fastest sustained speed of any battleship ever produced. The ships had an overall length of 887 ft 3 in, a full-load displacement of slightly more than 57,250 tons, and four sets of oil-fired steam turbines delivering 200,000 hp to four propeller shafts. The main battery had nine 16-in guns in triple turrets; the secondary battery included twenty 5-in guns in ten twin turrets; and the antiaircraft battery totaled between sixty and eighty 40-mm Bofors guns in quadruple mountings, and between forty-nine and sixty 20-mm cannon in single mountings.

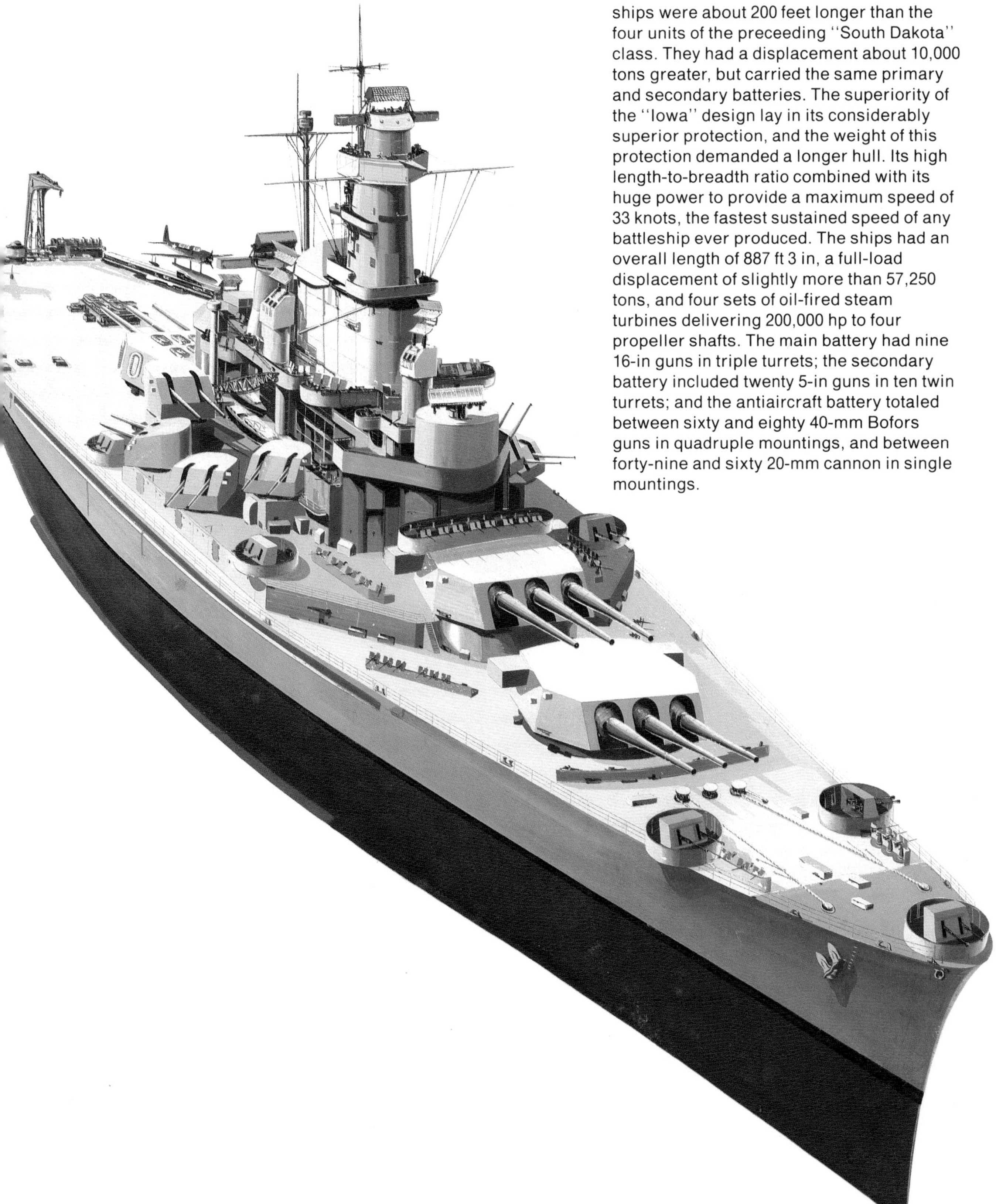

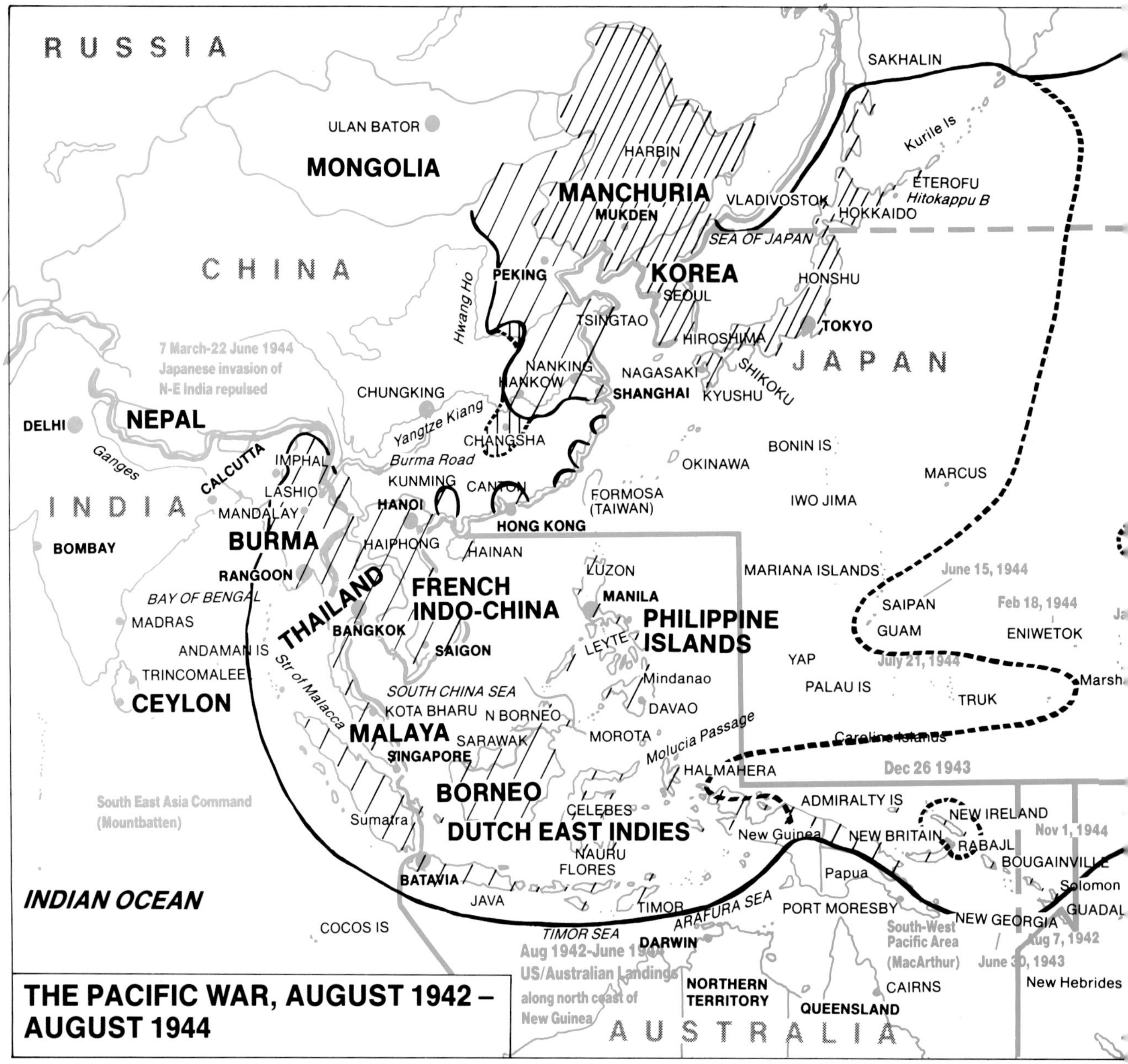

THE PACIFIC WAR, AUGUST 1942 – AUGUST 1944

Between August 1942 and August 1944, the Americans made serious inroads through Japan's defensive perimeter, and so paved the way for the reconquest of the Philippines.

destructive effect on the Japanese while at the same time improving the Allies' strategic position.

Army and navy planners therefore agreed on operations in New Guinea and the Solomon Islands. If they could close on Rabaul, they could eliminate the Japanese threat to the Americans' transpacific supply route at the same time. There was division about what should happen afterwards. MacArthur proposed a direct assault toward Rabaul via New Guinea using SWPA forces, with the navy playing a subordinate operational role. King and Nimitz proposed that an offensive along the line of the Solomon Islands should be followed by an invasion of New Britain from Bougainville, with the army playing the decidedly inferior role of garrisoning islands captured by the Navy and Marine Corps.

Mediation by Marshall

General Marshall believed MacArthur's plan was superior, but he had to mediate between MacArthur and King. On July 2, 1942, Marshall and King agreed a plan for the immediate elimination of the Japanese

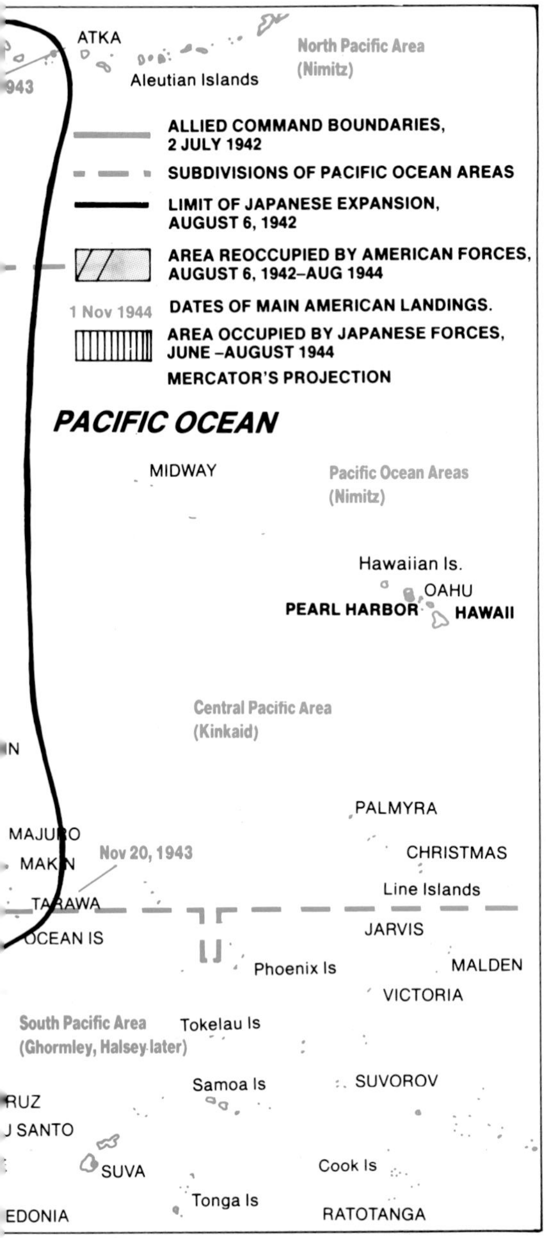

from New Guinea, New Britain, and New Ireland by joint army and navy forces.

Three Major Tasks

The operation was divided into three major tasks. In the first, forces of Vice Admiral Robert L. Ghormley's South Pacific Area, headquartered at Noumea in New Caledonia, would advance as early as possible in August to take the Santa Cruz Islands and the southeastern islands of the Solomons group where the Japanese had developed airfields. For this task, Ghormley would be reinforced by some of MacArthur's ships and aircraft. At the same time, aircraft from Australian bases would sever the Japanese air and naval lines of communication running into Ghormley's objective area. In the second task, MacArthur's SWPA forces would take the rest of the solomon Islands, the Japanese base area around Lae and Salamaua in Huon Gulf, and the northwest coast of New Guinea. These actions were regarded as a preliminary to the third task, which was also entrusted to the SWPA: the capture of Rabaul.

Within this overall scheme, the Joint Chiefs of Staff reserved the right to pull out any naval units after the completion of any task in case of an emergency elsewhere or the development of a particular threat to the aircraft carriers involved. In addition, the boundary between the SWPA and SPA was shifted slightly to the west. The islands of the Solomons group southeast from Santa Isabel now fell into the SPA's sphere of strategic responsibility.

Alexander A. Vandegrift was the major general commanding the 1st Marine Division in the hardest moments of the fighting for Guadalcanal.

Robert L. Ghormley
For further references see pages
42, 47, 49, 50

Guadalcanal
For further references see pages
42, *43*, 44, *45*, 46, *47*, 49, 50, 53, 54, 55, *56*

Local Objections

Both Ghormley and MacArthur objected that the plan was asking too much, too soon, and with too few resources. The JCS appreciated the two commanders' worries, but the discovery that the Japanese were building an airfield on Guadalcanal made them confirm the original scheme. Plans were pushed ahead with all speed, but shortage of the necessary shipping meant that the start of the first stage had to be postponed until August 7.

Ghormley disposed his force into three operational commands, namely the land-based support aircraft, the Amphibious Force (the assault convoy and its escort, the fire-support group, and the minesweepers), and the Air Support Force (three aircraft carriers escorted by a battleship, cruisers, and destroyers). On the morning of August 7, Rear Admiral Richmond K. Turner's Amphibious Force approached the southeastern Solomons, where landings were planned on Guadalcanal and Florida Island. Allied intelligence set the number of Japanese on the two islands at 5,000 on Guadalcanal and 2,000 on Florida, though the real totals appear to have been 2,230 and 1,500 including 1,700 and 600 labor troops respectively.

The Invasion of Guadalcanal

The assault by Major General Alexander A. Vandegrift's 1st Marine Division, reinforced to a strength of 19,000 men, took the japanese completely by surprise The four comparatively small landings on Florida and the two neighboring islets of Tulagi and Gavutu scattered the local Japanese forces, as did the major landing

Alexander Vandegrift
For further references see pages *41*, 43, 44, 45, 71

At the very beginning of a battle that was to be fought to a bitter conclusion and result in the first major land defeat for the Japanese in World War II, men of the 1st Marine Division advance landing party leave their landing craft and rush ashore into the cover provided by the jungle on Guadalcanal during August 7, 1942.

The main landing by the 1st Marine Division on Tulagi and Guadalcanal achieved complete surprise and was effectively unopposed.

on Guadalcanal. Vandegrift then moved the main strength of his division west toward Lunga Point and the airfield being built just to the south of it.

Vandegrift had relied on intelligence estimates and was unaware of how small the Japanese force on Guadalcanal really was. So, instead of expanding into the island to try to destroy the cohesion of the Japanese defenders, he committed his men to the establishment of a perimeter defense around Lunga Point and the airfield. Soon the transports lying between Guadalcanal and Florida were landing men and equipment as fast as they could. A taste of what was to come, however, was provided by Japanese air attacks on the Allied ships. These attacks soon grew in intensity and seriously impeded the unloading operation.

The Navy Pulls Out

As the days passed, the Japanese air and naval threat intensified. Under these circumstances, Admirals Fletcher and Turner decided that it was impossible to risk scarce American warships in such confined waters, and between August 9 and 19, the naval force was withdrawn. This left the 1st Marine Division short of supplies, and completely isolated on Guadalcanal and Florida. Long-range aircraft operating from the New Hebrides Islands could provide some air cover and fast destroyers were able to ferry in the most urgently needed supplies. On Guadalcanal itself, engineers hastily completed the airfield, which was named Henderson Field, and on August 20, a marine squadron of 31 aircraft moved into residence. Over the following weeks, marine air strength at Henderson Field was gradually increased to about 100 aircraft, which provided the marines with both air cover and direct air support.

During the same period, the Japanese were regrouping at Taivu Point and Kokumbona, east and west of Henderson Field. During the day, the "Slot," the channel between the northern and southern island chains of the Solomons, was dominated by Allied aircraft from

Richmond K. Turner
For further references see pages 42, 49, 53, 64, 76, 95

Henderson Field and the New Hebrides; but at night, the fast cruisers and destroyers of the "Tokyo Express" ran in. They encountered no effective resistance as they landed additional men and supplies on Guadalcanal before bombarding the marine positions and the airfield and finally dashing back to the northwest and comparative safety.

Occasional clashes took place between American and Japanese patrols, and they intensified from August 21 as the Japanese strength was revitalized by the efforts of the "Tokyo Express." By early September, Japanese forces on Guadalcanal had grown to about divisional strength, and between September 12 and 14 the Battle of Bloody Ridge erupted, when the Japanese tried to take Lunga Ridge, a position south of Henderson Field.

The Battle of Bloody Ridge

In the hands of the marines, the ridge was an essential part of the American perimeter around Henderson Field. In Japanese hands, it would have become a dominating height from which the Japanese could have brought the entire American position, including the airfield, under artillery fire. The Japanese launched a combination of infiltration and frontal attacks, and nearly broke through the marine positions before conceding defeat. Total Japanese losses are unknown, but 600 Japanese dead were found in the battlefield. American losses were 143 killed and wounded.

Smaller-scale fighting continued around the perimeter as both sides built up their strength. By mid-October, Vandegrift had 23,000 men under his command, and Japanese strength had risen to at least 20,000 men of Major General Haruyoshi Hyakutake's Japanese 17th Army, which added the Japanese 2nd Division and part of the Japanese 38th Division to the original forces in the island. Throughout the second half of September and the first half of October, the skirmishing and small-scale fighting

Men of the 43rd Infantry Division shelter on the very edge of Rendova Island during the landing of June 30, 1943. The landing was achieved during a torrential rainstorm. It secured artillery positions for the bombardment of New Georgia Island, the main target for the Americans in the central part of the Solomons.

became more frequent and also intensified as the Japanese prepared for a major effort to eliminate the American beachhead. The hard-pressed 1st Marine Division gave as good as it got, and from October 13 reinforcement arrived in the form of the 164th Infantry Regiment, the first unit of the U.S. Army's Americal Division to reach the island.

The major effort started on October 22. Over a period of three days, the Japanese launched a series of attacks right around the American perimeter. The fighting was extremely severe, but the Japanese failed to coordinate their efforts and came nowhere close to breaching the perimeter. When the battle ended on October 25, the Americans had lost less than 300 men, while the Japanese had suffered at least 2,000 killed and an unknown number wounded.

The Decisive Moment on Guadalcanal

Vandegrift realized that this had been the decisive moment in the Japanese attempt to drive the Allies back into the sea. From October 26, he extended the American perimeter far enough to prevent the Japanese artillery from hitting Henderson Field. Over the next six weeks, the boundary was steadily enlarged as the rest of the Americal Division and the 2nd Marine Division were landed to reinforce, and finally to relieve the exhausted 1st Marine Division.

On December 9, Vandegrift handed over responsibility for the Allied forces on Guadalcanal to Major General Alexander M. Patch, commander of the Americal Division, as the 1st Marine Division was evacuated to Australia. Between December 10 and January 9, 1943, the Allied strength on Guadalcanal was raised to 58,000 men, and on January 2 Patch became commander of the new XIV Corps that included the 2nd Marine, Americal, and 25th Infantry Divisions.

The Japanese now had less than 20,000 men on the island, and they were now both short of supplies and badly affected by disease. The Allies, on the other hand, were well supplied and affected comparatively little by disease. Their morale was also high after their success against earlier Japanese attacks, and they knew that the Japanese were now on the defensive.

The Allies Take the Offensive

On January 10, 1943, Patch committed XIV Corps to an offensive against the Japanese main position, which lay six miles west of Henderson Field and stretched from Point Cruz on the coast about four miles inland to the eastern slopes of Mount Austen. The 2nd Marine and 25th Infantry Divisions took the offensive against this position and were checked until January 23 by a defense of fanatical courage. Only on January 23 did the Americans break through as the Japanese fell back under cover of a very well-conducted rearguard action. The Japanese attempted to halt the Americans at the Bonegi River, which runs into the sea at Tassafaronga Point, but on January 31, they were driven back toward Cape Esperance.

In an effort to prevent the escape of the Japanese by sea, the 2nd Battalion of the 132nd Infantry Regiment landed in the Japanese rear at Verahue before advancing northeast along the coast toward Cape Esperance. In a quite remarkable feat, however, the Japanese navy managed to evacuate 13,000 soldiers between February 1 and 7.

The importance of the American land victory at Guadalcanal cannot be overemphasized. It was the first major land defeat suffered by the Japanese army at the hands of the Allies. Both sides made serious mistakes during the campaign, but the Japanese made the worst mistake when they failed to use their initial air, land, and sea superiority to sweep the Allies back into the sea in the first two months of the campaign. Thereafter the Japanese failed to exploit their strength, wasting it instead on piecemeal attacks as the Allies built up an overwhelming superiority.

The Guadalcanal Naval Campaign

Throughout the land campaign for Guadalcanal, a series of naval battles had

Men of the 1st Marine Division man an M1 75-mm pack howitzer on Guadalcanal. This light howitzer fired its 13·76-lb shell to a maximum range of only 9,760 yards, but shell weight and range were more than adequate for the area, where its light weight and maneuverability were more important. In any event, the shell weight and range were adequate for the nature of the fighting on Guadalcanal.

been fought that had a significant effect on the course of operations not only in the Solomons but in New Guinea and elsewhere. The first of these clashes was the Battle of Savo Island on August 9, and its outcome precipitated the naval withdrawal that left the 1st Marine Division so isolated at the beginning of the campaign.

The Battle of Savo Island

Under the command of Vice Admiral Gunichi Mikawa, a Japanese force of seven cruisers and one destroyer passed through the strait (soon known as Ironbottom Sound for the number of ships at the bottom of it) between Guadalcanal and Florida, and completely surprised the patrolling Allied heavy cruisers (four American and one Australian) under a British officer, Rear Admiral Crutchley. In just 32 minutes of superb ship handling and night gunfire, the Japanese sank four of the cruisers, together with a destroyer, and severely damaged the last cruiser. Mikawa thought that the Allies still had aircraft carriers in the area and therefore retired well before dawn without attempting to attack the now helpless invasion transports lying off Guadalcanal and Florida. The Japanese ships had suffered only light damage, resulting in the deaths of 37 men killed and 57 wounded, but the heavy cruiser *Kako* was then sunk by the American submarine *S-44* as she headed back toward Rabaul. The Allies suffered 1,270 killed and 709 wounded, with the Battle of Savo Island arguably the most humiliating defeat ever suffered by the U.S. Navy in a fair fight.

On August 22, the Japanese decided to run a convoy of three transports with 1,500 soldiers to Guadalcanal. This reinforcement operation was led by Rear Admiral Raizo Tanaka, whose Convoy Escort Force totaled one light cruiser and eight destroyers. The importance of the reinforcement convoy is clear from the strength of the surface and air support provided by elements of the Combined Fleet arriving from Truk. There were two formations of the 3rd Fleet (the two fleet carriers *Shokaku* and *Zuikaku*, and six destroyers of Nagumo's Carrier Strike Force, and the single light carrier *Ryujo*, single heavy cruiser, and two destroyers of Rear Admiral Chuichi Hara's Detached Carrier Strike Force) and several formations of the 2nd Fleet and Vice Admiral Kondo's 8th Fleet (including the two battleships, three heavy cruisers, one light cruiser, and three destroyers of Rear Admiral Koso Abe's Vanguard Force and the five heavy cruisers, one light cruiser, six destroyers, and one seaplane tender of Kondo's Support Force).

The Japanese were not sure whether their naval codes were being read by the Allies, but had decided to change them.

Even so, American intelligence deduced from the quantity and geographical spread of Japanese naval radio traffic that a major operation was imminent. Ghormley responded by sending Vice Admiral Fletcher's TF61, which included three subordinate task forces with the fleet carriers *Enterprise*, *Saratoga*, and U.S.S. *Wasp*, one battleship, five heavy cruisers, two light cruisers, and 18 destroyers. As a result of faulty intelligence, however, Fletcher detached the Wasp group to refuel, and in the resulting clash, he had only two fleet carriers available.

The Battle of the Eastern Solomons

The Battle of the Eastern Solomons began on August 23 in the open waters north of Guadalcanal and its neighbors. American aircraft soon sank the *Ryujo*, whose own aircraft were attacking Henderson Field, but on August 24, the *Shokaku*'s and *Zuikaku*'s aircraft attacked the *Enterprise* and severely damaged her. Then, they switched their attentions to the *Saratoga*, which suffered no damage, and her fighters downed a substantial number of Japanese attackers, which were also hit by the heavy antiaircraft armament of the new battleship U.S.S. *South Carolina*. The *Saratoga*'s attack aircraft found and badly damaged the seaplane tender *Chitose*, but could not find the main Japanese strength.

Fletcher now pulled back after suffering the loss of only 17 aircraft and damage to the *Enterprise*. Kondo ordered a pursuit, but then broke it off. The Japanese had lost were 90 aircraft, the *Ryujo* had lost 90 aircraft, the *Ryujo* had been sunk, and the *Chitose* had delivered his soldiers, bombarded Henderson Field, and pulled back. The following day his force was found by American aircraft, which sank one destroyer and damaged Tanaka's flagship, the light cruiser *Jintsu*. The Battle of the Eastern Solomons was neither won nor lost, but the Japanese suffered considerably higher aircraft losses.

The *Saratoga* was damaged by torpedo attack on August 31 and was out of

Four Mitsubishi G4M bombers, known to the Allies by the reporting name "Betty," run the gauntlet of U.S. antiaircraft fire as they make a torpedo attack on the anchorage at Lunga Roads off Guadalcanal. The aircraft on the extreme left and right are only about 15 feet above the water.

Marine, U.S. Marine Corps, Guadalcanal, Winter, 1942-43

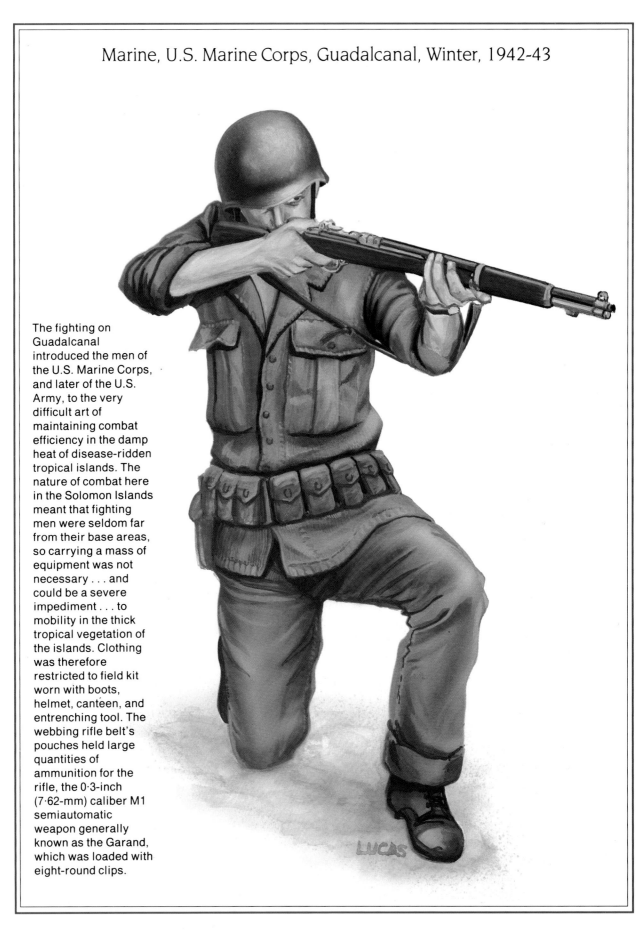

The fighting on Guadalcanal introduced the men of the U.S. Marine Corps, and later of the U.S. Army, to the very difficult art of maintaining combat efficiency in the damp heat of disease-ridden tropical islands. The nature of combat here in the Solomon Islands meant that fighting men were seldom far from their base areas, so carrying a mass of equipment was not necessary . . . and could be a severe impediment . . . to mobility in the thick tropical vegetation of the islands. Clothing was therefore restricted to field kit worn with boots, helmet, canteen, and entrenching tool. The webbing rifle belt's pouches held large quantities of ammunition for the rifle, the 0·3-inch (7·62-mm) caliber M1 semiautomatic weapon generally known as the Garand, which was loaded with eight-round clips.

A Boeing B-17F Flying Fortress bomber is seen at unusually low level during a raid on Gizo Island, northwest of New Georgia Island in the central Solomons, October 5, 1942.

action for three months as repairs were made. At this time, the only U.S. carrier in the Pacific was the *Wasp*, and she was lost just over two weeks later.

Ghormley felt that the 1st Marine division on Guadalcanal had to be reinforced. The 7th Marine Regiment was sent forward from Espiritu Santo in the New Hebrides on September 14 in six transports escorted by the Pacific Fleet's depleted carrier strength. On September 15, this force was intercepted by two Japanese submarines. The *I-15* damaged the *North Carolina* and sank a submarine, while the *I-19* torpedoed and sank the *Wasp*. Turner pressed ahead with the transports and reached Guadalcanal on September 18. Both sides were now bolstering their forces on Guadalcanal, and the next American and Japanese efforts clashed head-on in the Battle of Cape Esperance.

The Battle of Cape Esperance

Between October 11 and 13, Turner ran the 164th Infantry Regiment into the island in two large transports and eight destroyer transports escorted by Rear Admiral Norman Scott's TF64 (two heavy cruisers, two light cruisers, and five destroyers). At the same time, the Japanese were running a convoy of two seaplane tenders and six destroyers loaded with men and equipment down the "Slot." They were escorted by Rear Admiral Arimoto Goto's Bombardment Force of the Outer South Sea Force (three heavy cruisers and two destroyers). Intelligence warned Scott of the Japanese movement. Scott intercepted Goto's force and, in a night action illuminated by American aircraft, sank one cruiser and one destroyer while severely damaging two other cruisers. Both troop convoys landed their men and supplies safely, but American aircraft sank two Japanese destroyers as the convoy pulled back toward Rabaul.

Between October 13 and 15, the bombardment of Henderson Field, first by Japanese battleships and then by Japanese destroyers, indicated that Japan had succeeded in re-establishing command of the sea around Guadalcanal. On

October 18, Ghormley was replaced at the head of the SPA by Vice Admiral Halsey. At much the same time, Fletcher was succeeded by Rear Admiral Thomas C. Kinkaid as commander of the American carrier strength, made up of the *Hornet* and the repaired *Enterprise*.

Yamamoto had meanwhile decided on a major effort to secure total Japanese domination of the waters around the Solomons and had allocated to Kondo's 2nd Fleet two fleet and two light carriers with which to score a decisive victory over the U.S. Navy. Yamamoto was unwilling to commit his precious carriers unless he had a land base to provide a haven for his pilots and aircraft should their carriers be sunk and allow land-based bomber support to be deployed. The Japanese army assured Yamamoto that its reinforced strength on Guadalcanal would soon recover Henderson Field, and Yamamoto allowed Kondo's 2nd Fleet to advance from Truk in the Caroline Islands at about the same time that Kinkaid's TF16 and TF17 were circling around to the north of the Santa Cruz Islands.

In addition to the two fleet and two light carriers, the Japanese had four battleships, eight heavy cruisers, two light cruisers, 30 destroyers, and 12 submarines. The Allies deployed two fleet carriers, one battleship, three heavy cruisers, three light cruisers, and 14 destroyers.

Thomas Kinkaid

For further references see pages 53, 112

The Battle of the Santa Cruz Islands

As the last major effort was being made by the Japanese on Guadalcanal to recapture Henderson Field and push the Americans back into the sea, Halsey ordered Kinkaid to take the war to the Japanese. The result was the Battle of the Santa Cruz Islands, fought on October 26 and 27. The two forces launched their aircraft at about the same time. The attacking formations passed in mid-air, and several of the American aircraft were

A U.S. aircraft carrier with an escorting destroyer. The naval war in the Pacific was essentially a war between the seaborne aircraft of America and Japan. The numerical advantage of the U.S. aircraft carriers made the final outcome of the fight almost guaranteed.

Top: The classic pincer attack of naval air power is seen in action as the fleet carrier *Hornet* comes under such attack during the Battle of the Santa Cruz Islands on October 26, 1942. The pincer attack involved simultaneous attacks by torpedo and dive bombers (in this instance Nakajima B5N "Kate" and Aichi D3A "Val" aircraft respectively), so that the target could not maneuver to avoid both. In this ten-minute attack, the *Hornet* suffered a bomb hit on the flight deck; a Japanese plane crashed through the funnel and the flight deck before its two bombs exploded; two torpedo hits in the engine room halted the ship; three more bombs hit, including two that penetrated the flight deck and exploded four decks deeper; and finally another crashing plane hit and destroyed the forward aircraft elevator. The ship was taken in tow and later abandoned by most of her non-essential crew. She was then attacked and hit by Japanese aircraft in another four attacks, completely abandoned and torpedoed four times by American destroyers, and finally sunk by torpedoes from two Japanese destroyers the following day.

Left: The funnel and signals bridge of the *Hornet* were devastated in the fleet carrier's ordeal

Above: Despite damage that caused her to list to port, the fleet carrier *Enterprise* was still able to operate her air group during the Battle of the Santa Cruz Islands. Here, deck crew reposition aircraft in preparation for takeoff, while overhead, four fighters depart.

Right: Accidents were not uncommon during flight deck operations. Here, the catapult officer scrambles up onto a blazing Grumman F6F Hellcat fighter in an effort to rescue a pilot who had come to grief while landing on the fleet carrier Enterprise en route to the Gilbert Islands invasion of November 1943.

shot down by Japanese fighters. In the following attacks, the Americans damaged the light carrier *Zuiho* and severely damaged the *Shokaku*, which was out of action for nine months. The Japanese were more successful, hitting the *Hornet* so hard that she had to be towed out of action by a cruiser, and then severely damaging the *Enterprise* with a second wave of attackers launched from the two surviving Japanese carriers. The Allies were compelled to pull back, and

Right: Admiral Isoroku Yamamoto was commander-in-chief of the Combined Fleet until his death on April 18, 1943. Although he was in many ways a brilliant and far-sighted commander, Yamamoto had a major operational failing. He created vastly complex, and ultimately unworkable, battle plans.

the *Hornet* was abandoned to be sunk by Japanese destroyers. Kondo then retired to the north after winning a tactical victory, but it was also a serious Japanese reverse as another 100 aircraft and their crews had been lost. The Allies lost about 50 aircraft.

The Battle of Guadalcanal

The next engagement, the Battle of Guadalcanal, which lasted from November 12 to 15, was the most complex naval action of the campaign. Again, the event that triggered the battle was a Japanese reinforcement convoy, this time carrying 13,000 men in 11 transports escorted by Tanaka's Escort Force of 11 destroyers. Cover for this vital convoy was provided by Kondo's 2nd Fleet, which used varying formations for the different phases of the battle. At the same time, the Americans ran their own reinforcement convoy of four transports escorted by Rear Admiral Daniel J. Callaghan's Task Group 67.4 (three heavy cruisers, two light cruisers, and seven destroyers) into Guadalcanal.

In the first phase of the battle, Kondo sought to distract Allied attention from the troop convoy by shelling Henderson Field. This task was entrusted to Abe's Raiding Advance Force (two battleships, one light cruiser, and 14 destroyers), with air cover provided by the carrier *Junyo* and her escorts well to the north of the Solomons.

The Allies discovered the approach of Tanaka's and Abe's forces, and Callaghan secured Turner's approval to intercept. The damaged *Enterprise*, with a tender lashed alongside making repairs as they moved, was making all the speed she could toward the area, but was still too far away for her aircraft to intervene. Turner and Callaghan therefore planned to use surprise to offset their numerical inferiority.

Even though the American ships had radar and those of the Japanese did not, it was Abe who surprised Callaghan on entering Ironbottom Sound in the early hours of the morning. A very confused 36-minute action followed as the two forces engaged each other, often at pointblank range. The Japanese battleship *Hiei* was left helpless (and was sunk by aircraft from the *Enterprise*'s air group as they headed for Henderson Field the following day), the destroyers *Akatsuki* and *Yudachi* were sunk, and all the other Japanese ships were damaged. The Americans lost the heavy cruiser U.S.S. *Portland* and the light cruiser U.S.S. *Juneau*. Four destroyers were sunk, another cruiser and destroyer very badly damaged, and all other ships but one damaged. Admirals Callaghan and Scott were both killed. Abe abandoned the bombardment of Henderson Field, and Tanaka's convoy returned to Shortland Island, leaving the Allies victorious.

The second phase of the battle was fought the following day. After a period of intense air activity, Tanaka headed southeast from Shortland during the day in another effort to reach Guadalcanal. After dark, a Japanese force of three heavy cruisers and two destroyers under Vice Admiral Gunichi Mikawa entered Ironbottom Sound and shelled Henderson Field. During the following morning, American aircraft found both Japanese forces, sinking seven of Tanaka's ships and one of Mikawa's heavy cruisers, and causing severe damage to other Mikawa's ships.

Tanaka continued toward Guadalcanal with his surviving ships, which were carrying elements of the Japanese 38th Division, and Kondo moved to support Tanaka by bombarding Henderson Field with a force of one battleship, two heavy cruisers, two light cruisers, and nine destroyers. Kinkaid was still too far away

The wreck of the Japanese transport *Kinugawa Maru* on Munda Island off New Georgia in November 1943. The sea battles in and around the Solomon Islands tested both sides to their limits, but the combination of American sea and air power combined eventually reduced the Japanese to the use of light cruisers and destroyers in high-speed night passages in an effort to reinforce, supply, and finally evacuate their otherwise isolated garrisons.

to intervene directly with the *Enterprise*, but sent Rear Admiral Willis A. Lee's TG64 (two battleships and four destroyers) to intercept Kondo's Attack Force.

The third phase of the battle, fought in the night of November 14/15, was another close-range engagement just south of Savo Island. Two of the American destroyers were sunk almost immediately, and the other two were rapidly disabled. Lee closed in with his two battleships, the U.S.S. *Washington* and the *South Dakota*. The Japanese concentrated their fire on the *South Dakota*, which suffered total electrical failure and was knocked out of the battle. Not deterred despite the fact that he was now faced by 14 Japanese warships, Lee concentrated the *Washington*'s radar-controlled guns on the *Kirishima*. The Japanese battleship was reduced to a floating wreck and soon sank, together with the destroyer *Ayanami*.

The Battle of Guadalcanal gave control of the waters around Guadalcanal to the Allies, and so was a major plank in the eventual American triumph in the whole campaign.

The Battles of Tassafaronga and Rennell's Island

Even so, there were two more naval engagements in the campaign. On November 30, the Battle of Tassafaronga resulted in a clearcut Japanese tactical victory. Tanaka was again running a "Tokyo Express" operation into Guadalcanal, this time with eight destroyers. Warned by radar of Tanaka's approach, Rear Admiral Carleton H. Wright was waiting with the five cruisers and seven destroyers of TF67. The Americans opened fire too soon, and as they reversed course, the Japanese unleashed a torpedo salvo that sank the heavy cruiser U.S.S. *Northampton* and severely damaged three other American cruisers.

The Japanese lost only one destroyer.

The last naval action of the Guadalcanal campaign was the Battle of Rennell's Island on January 29/30, 1943. As Japanese naval forces gathered in the northwestern Solomons for the evacuation of the last Japanese soldiers from Guadalcanal, the Allies unwisely tried to tempt them into battle against Rear Admiral Robert C. Giffin's force of two escort carriers, six cruisers, and eight destroyers. The Japanese refused the bait, but Yamamoto responded with two successful land-based air attacks. The first disabled the heavy cruiser U.S.S. *Chicago*, and the second sank her.

Operations in New Guinea

As the operations on and around Guadalcanal were breaching this portion of the Japanese perimeter and so completing the first part of the American strategic plan, MacArthur's SWPA forces were undertaking the second task.

From July 21, 1942, Major General Tomitoro Horii's Japanese 18th Army had moved inland from its beachhead at Gona, pushing back the Allied defense and moving up the Kokoda Trail to reach the pass over the Owen Stanley Mountains on August 12. Pushing forward despite its lack of supplies and the increasing occurrence of disease, the Japanese 18th Army got within 30 miles of Port Moresby before it was stopped by an American and Australian force on September 13. An earlier Japanese attempt to take Milne Bay at the eastern end of New Guinea had been defeated by Australian units sensibly located in the area by MacArthur.

Between September and November 1942, the Japanese 18th Army fell back across the Owen Stanley Mountains under pressure from two Allied formations, the 32nd Infantry Division and the Australian 7th Division. The Allied advance was finally checked on November 19 outside the fortress area constructed by the Japanese in the swampy region inland from Buna and Gona. From November 20, the two divisions tried to fight their way into this fortress area, but were soon stalled. This was due in part to

Previous page top: A marine sniper climbs a palm on Guadalcanal. The vantage point offered by such a perch was good, but the tree offered little concealment.

Previous page below: A soldier catches a brief rest on a dump of 155-mm shells on Rendova Island. At the front of each shell is a lifting ring, which was unscrewed and replaced by the fuse when the shell was to be fired.

the staunch Japanese defense, but also to disease, a shortage of supplies, inadequate artillery, and lack of the tactical skills needed to fight the Japanese in such terrain.

The Battle for Buna and Gona

The Allied force soon lost the last vestiges of its morale, and on December 1 MacArthur sent Lieutenant General Robert L. Eichelberger to replace Lieutenant General Herring as commander of the Advanced New Guinea Force. Eichelberger soon boosted Allied morale, largely by improving the logistical network that allowed the inward flow of supplies and equipment as well as the outward flow of the wounded and the ill. Eichelberger also replaced Major General Edwin F. Harding, commander of the 32nd Infantry Division with Brigadier General Albert W. Waldron, at the same time replacing the commanders of the division's two subordinate units, the Urbana and Warren Forces.

On December 9, the Australian 7th Division stormed Gona, the less well-protected Japanese position, and so freed the Allied left from fear of Japanese interference from Buna. But Buna was an altogether tougher nut to crack. The Americans and Australians fought their way forward yard by yard. On January 3, the Buna beachhead had been destroyed by the Americans with Australian support, while the last Japanese toehold at Sanananda was cleared on January 22 by the Australians with support from the 163rd Infantry Regiment of the 41st Infantry Division.

Japanese losses are estimated at between 13,000 and 15,000, including at least 7,000 dead. The Australians suffered 5,700 killed and wounded; and the American figure was 2,783, from a total of 13,646 men involved. In addition, another 2,334 Americans were incapacitated by disease. This operation was in fact the first success by Allied forces against the Japanese, preceding the larger victory on Guadalcanal. In addition to showing for the first time that the Allies could beat the Japanese in a land campaign, the fighting also provided the Allies with invaluable experience in the nature of Japanese defensive systems and the tactical methods necessary to overcome them.

The Japanese Replan their Defense

In the first weeks of 1943, the Japanese reorganized their defensive perimeter to take account of Allied successes in New Guinea and on Guadalcanal. These Allied victories were a clear threat to the perimeter's southeast quadrant, so the forces based on Rabaul were strengthened to improve the defensive capabilities between the Huon Gulf in New Guinea and New Georgia Island in the central Solomons. This whole sector was under the naval command of Vice Admiral Jinichi Kosaka, whose subordinate army formation was Lieutenant General Hitoshi Imamura's Japanese 8th Area Army, which in turn controlled Lieutenant General Hitoshi Imamura's Japanese 18th Army in New Guinea and Lieutenant General Iwao Matsuda's Japanese 17th Army in the Solomons. This southeastern quadrant offered the greatest threat to Japan's entire defensive strategy, so close supervision was exercised by Yamamoto, whose Combined Fleet headquarters was located at Truk.

The Japanese at first thought that these strengthened forces would allow them to recapture Guadalcanal Island and successfully complete the overland advance on Port Moresby. However, the Allied success at Buna combined with the final American victory on Guadalcanal convinced the Japanese that this initial plan was too optimistic, and in February 1943 they decided to base the defense of the quadrant on the Huon Gulf in the west and New Georgia Island in the east.

Emphasis Switches from the SPA to the SWPA

As far as the Allies were concerned, the focus of attention was now shifting from the first to the second task of the July 1942 strategic plan. As Rabaul was now the primary objective, much of the SPA's air, land, amphibious, and naval strength

Rabaul
For further references see pages
58, 59, *64*, 65, 72, 73, 88, 89

Commander, U.S. Navy, 1943

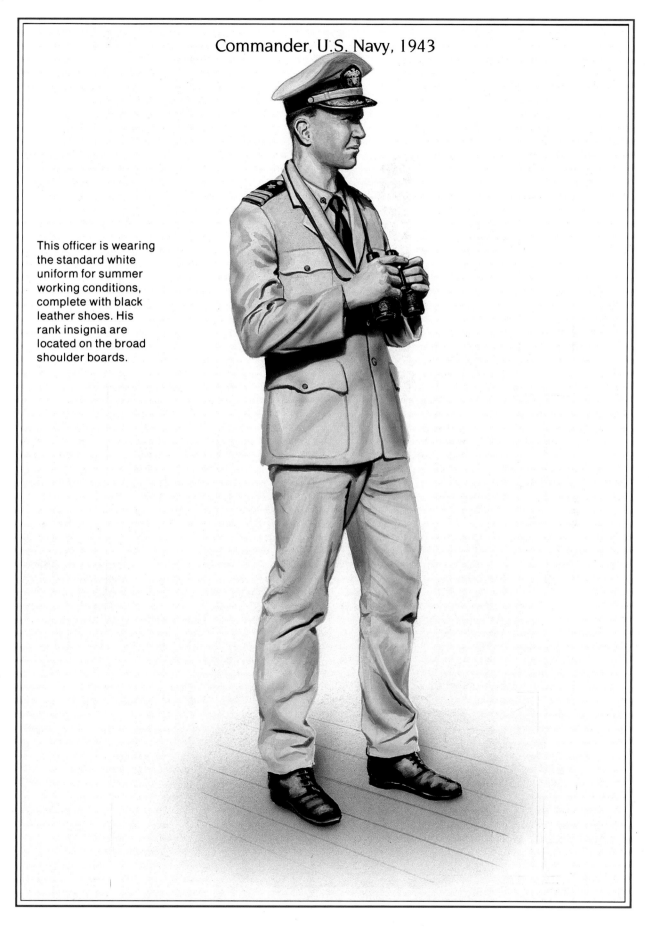

This officer is wearing the standard white uniform for summer working conditions, complete with black leather shoes. His rank insignia are located on the broad shoulder boards.

was shifted to the SWPA to allow a coordinated two-prong offensive toward Rabaul.

It was clear that, without considerable reinforcement, the SWPA would not be able to complete the second task by the end of 1943 as originally envisaged. The Casablanca Conference had decided that the SWPA would not receive reinforcement on the scale demanded by MacArthur; in March 1943, MacArthur proposed a revised, less ambitious operational plan, which was accepted in April as the "Cartwheel" program. Within this revised plan, which came under MacArthur's strategic control, Halsey's forces were to advance northwest up the line of the Solomons. They would take Bougainville Island by the end of the year, as the jumping-off point for New Ireland, while the Australian New Guinea Force, supported by American formations, advanced northwest through New Guinea to pave the way for General Walter Krueger's 6th Army to jump across the Vitiaz Strait and land in the western part of New Britain.

The plan was sound in concept, but problems occurred because Halsey's forces still depended for ships, troops, aircraft, and logistics on the Pacific Ocean Areas, where Nimitz had other priorities. The fact that the two offensives worked so well is a great testament to the effective working relationship developed by MacArthur and Halsey.

MacArthur's Renewed Offensive

Starting on January 9, the Japanese tried to take the existing mountain airfield at Wau. The site would have provided their air forces with an ideal position for fighters to attack Allied bombers heading toward the Japanese coastal positions, and for bombers to raid Allied positions. MacArthur already had designs on this tactically important airfield, and on January 29 the Japanese were forestalled by the arrival of an airlifted Australian brigade. Wau, only 30 miles west of Salamaua, was an effective forward base that threatened Japan's coastal garrisons.

New Guinea offered a desperately bad combination of climate, terrain, and disease for American soldiers such as the patrol seen here.

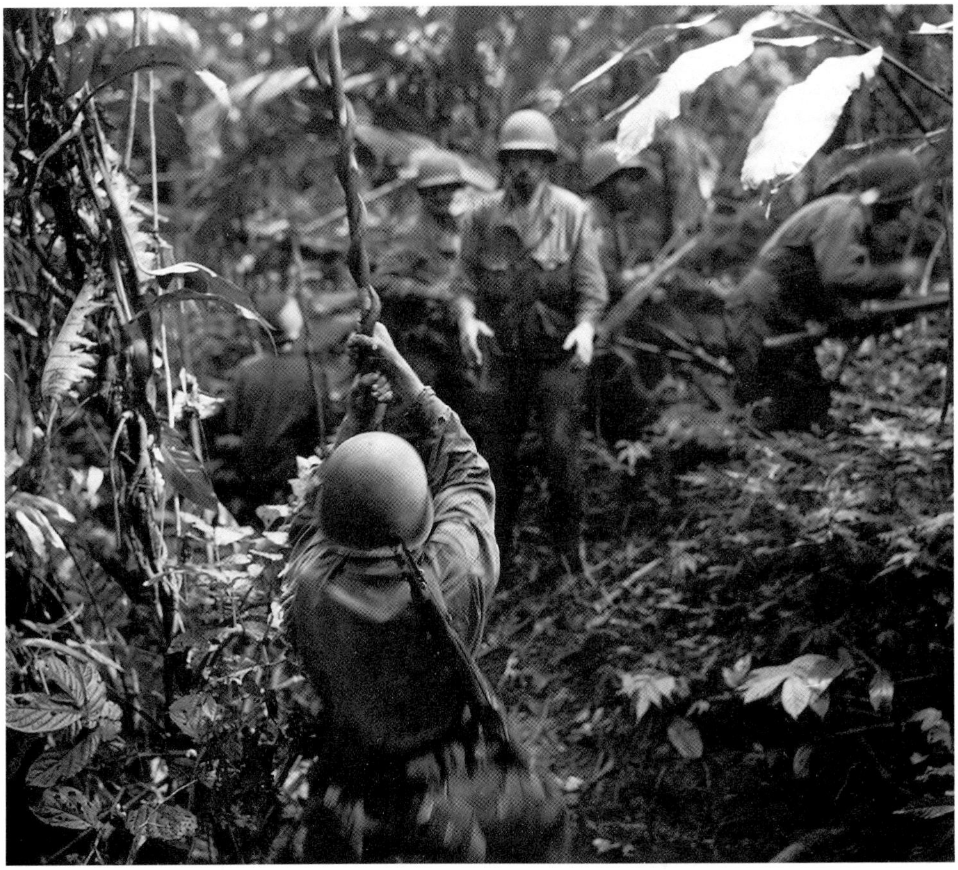

The Battle of the Bismarck Sea

At the beginning of march, the Japanese tried to reinforce Lae and Salamaua with 6,900 soldiers moved by sea from Rabaul. The convoy of eight transports was escorted by eight destroyers, but it was detected by the Allies on March 2. The resulting Battle of the Bismarck Sea was a resounding success of Allied air power, in the form of Lieutenant General George C. Kennedy's 5th Army Air Force. Using B-25 Mitchell medium bombers with a "solid" nose accommodating a heavy battery of machine guns to strafe the Japanese ships' decks, the Americans attacked with the newly developed skip bombing technique. A bomb dropped at very low level bounced horizontally off the water into the target's side before exploding on or just above the waterline, deep in its bowels. The Battle of the Bismarck Sea cost the Allies two bombers and three fighters, in addition to 25 aircraft, the Japanese lost seven transports and four destroyers to air attack, and the last transport to PT boat attack. The four other destroyers limped back to Rabaul with extensive damage, and more than 3,000 Japanese soldiers drowned.

After this disastrous episode, the Japanese used only fast destroyers to run reinforcements and supplies into their New Guinea coastal garrisons.

By now, the Allies had realized that the best way to defeat the Japanese was not by frontal assault on their prepared defenses, but by using air and sea superiority to bypass the main positions, which were then isolated and attacked from the flanks or rear.

The cautious sergeant checks that a Japanese strongpoint on New Guinea has been properly cleared. The Japanese matched their cleverness in creating such strongpoints out of local materials with considerable cunning. They sometimes "played dead" until the Americans were off guard, whereupon they would "come to life" and open fire.

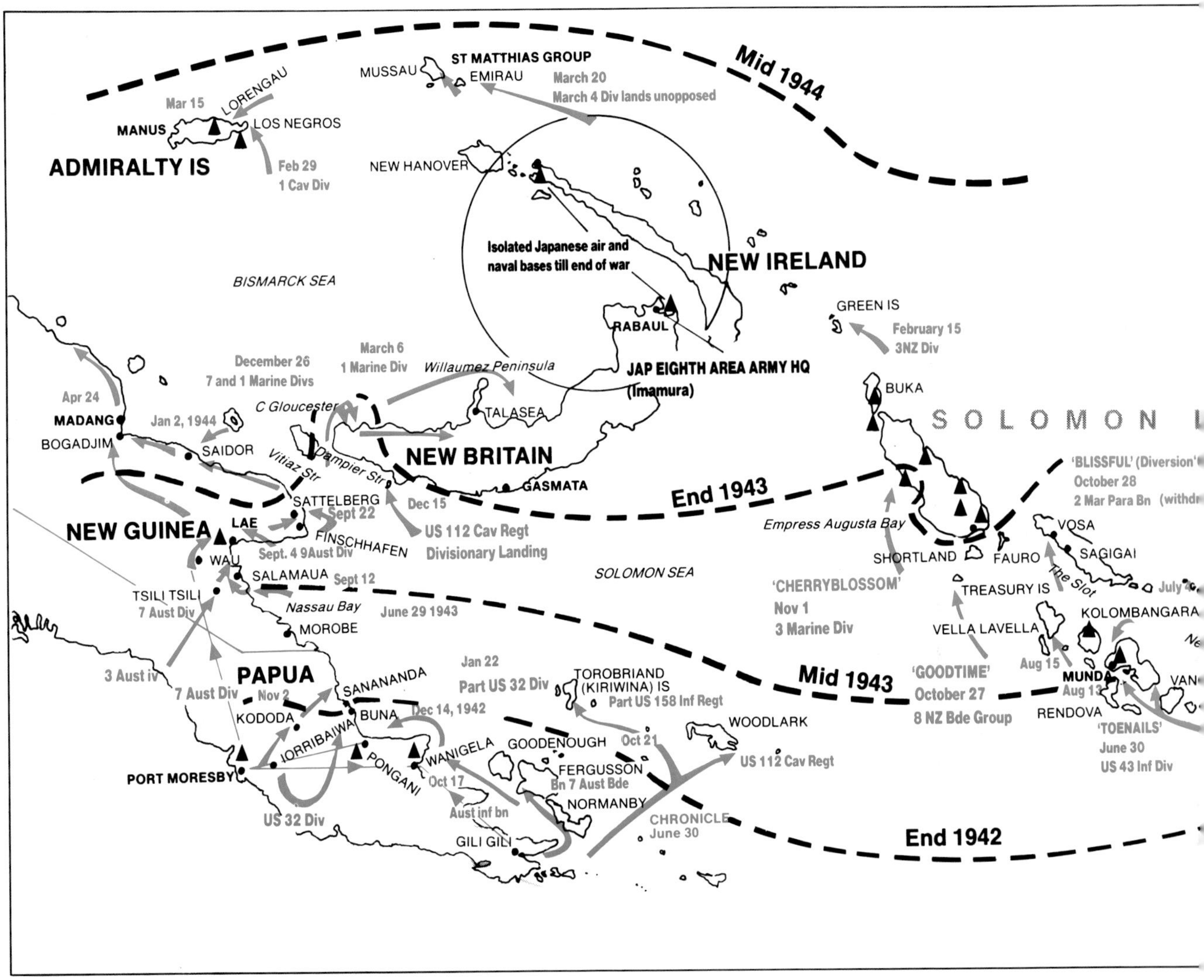

The U.S. and Australian operations in the Solomons and New Guinea closed steadily round the Japanese base areas on New Britain and New Ireland.

This technique was first used to capture Salamaua and Lae, Japan's main bases in the Huon Gulf. On the night of June 29/30, a detachment of the 32nd Infantry Division landed at Nassau Bay, just down the coast from Salamaua, and convinced the Japanese that the main attack would come from the southeast.

At the same time, elements of the 6th Army were escorted by units of Vice Admiral A. S. Carpenter's 7th Fleet on their way to take the Trobriad and Woodland Islands, north of New Guinea's eastern tip. New airfields were quickly prepared, giving additional bases to the rapidly growing Allied air strength.

These operations paved the way for the massive offensive against Salamaua and Lae in September by the forces of General Sir Thomas Blamey's New Guinea Force under MacArthur's direct supervision. On September 4, the Australian 9th Division landed east of Lae, between the mouth of the Buso River and Hopoi. The following day, the 503rd Parachute Infantry Regiment was dropped at Nadzab, northwest of Lae in the lower part of the Markham River valley. The 503rd PIR was immediately reinforced by the Australian 7th Division, airlifted from Port Morseby, and the Allies began to close on Lae from two directions. With the attention of the Japanese focused on Lae, the detachment of the 32nd Division at Nassau Bay moved forward against Salamaua, while the Australian 3rd Division advanced east toward the same target

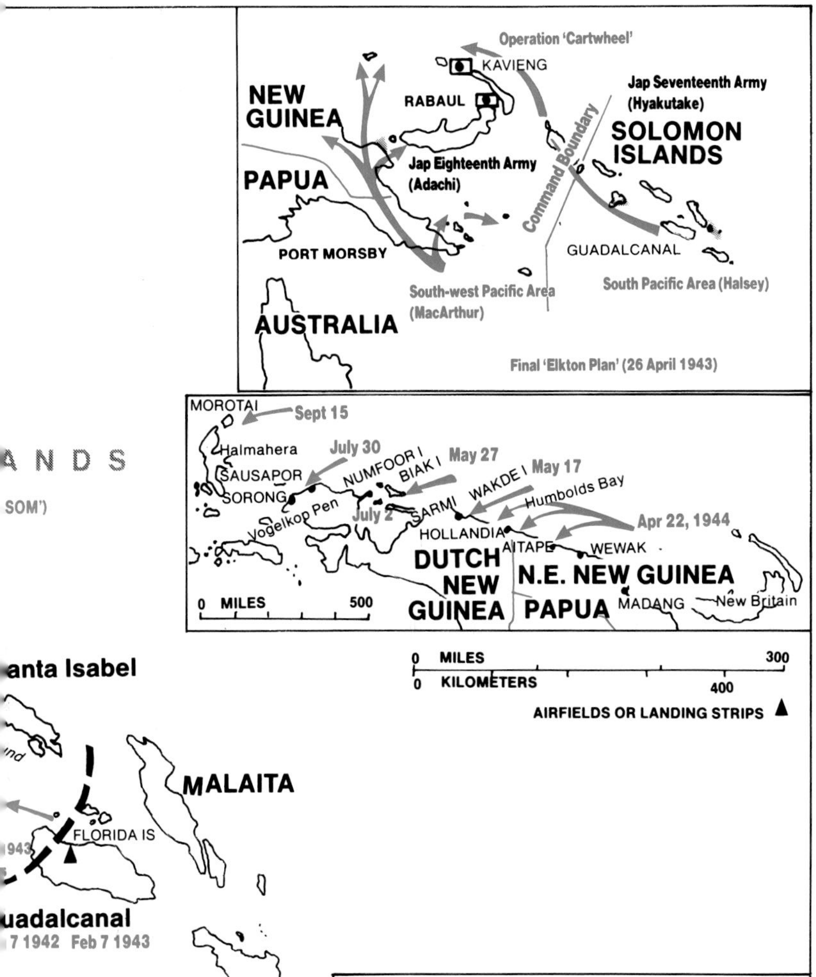

THE OFFENSIVES IN THE SOLOMONS AND NEW GUINEA

from Wau. The Japanese saw that neither place could be held and abandoned them. Salamaua was taken on September 12, and Lae fell four days later.

MacArthur saw an ideal opportunity for rapid exploitation, and on September 22, he moved into the Huon peninsula with ground and amphibious assaults. Finschhafen was encircled on the first day and fell on October 2.

The whole campaign had been an excellent example of combined air, land and sea operations, in which tactical air operations came of age in the Pacific theater. At the same time, the Australian 7th Division moved up the Markham River valley toward Gusa and then down the Ramu River to Dumpu. Here the division was replaced by the Australian 11th Division, which set off toward the coast at Bogadjim over the Kankiryo Saddle of the Finisterre Mountains. This movement, completed only in April 1944, succeeded, with Australian progress around the coast and American amphibious operations against Saidor in January 1944, and Yalau Plantation in March 1944, in isolating the Huon peninsula.

The Role of Tactical Air Power

Tactical air operations were the responsibility of the 5th AAF. They remained essentially unaltered for the rest of the Pacific campaign and played a decisive part in the succession of American victories. Fighters and light bombers used in the first phase of these tactics gained complete air superiority over an area by attacking airfields. They also used their increasing technical and tactical superiority to destroy Japanese aircraft in the air. At the same time, longer-range bombers attacked and neutralized more distant air bases from which the Japanese might intervene. Heavier bombers were often aided by land- and carrier-based aircraft of the South and/or Central Pacific Areas.

In the second phase, fighters and bombers isolated the operational area in question, making it impossible for the Japanese to deliver reinforcements or supplies by air or sea. In the third phase, all available tactical aircraft gave support to any forces involved in the land, airborne or amphibious battle by intensifying attacks on Japanese tactical positions and maintaining them until the Japanese had been defeated. A related by parallel task was airborne operations. Troop-carrier aircraft flew paratroopers to their objective, usually an airfield or a flat area where an airfield could be developed quickly. The aircraft flew shuttle missions to ferry in troops and equipment. Among the first troops to be airlifted were combat engineers, who improved and expanded the captured airfield or created a new one, so that fighters and then light bombers could be flown in to provide ground forces with tactical air support.

These forward airfields also supported

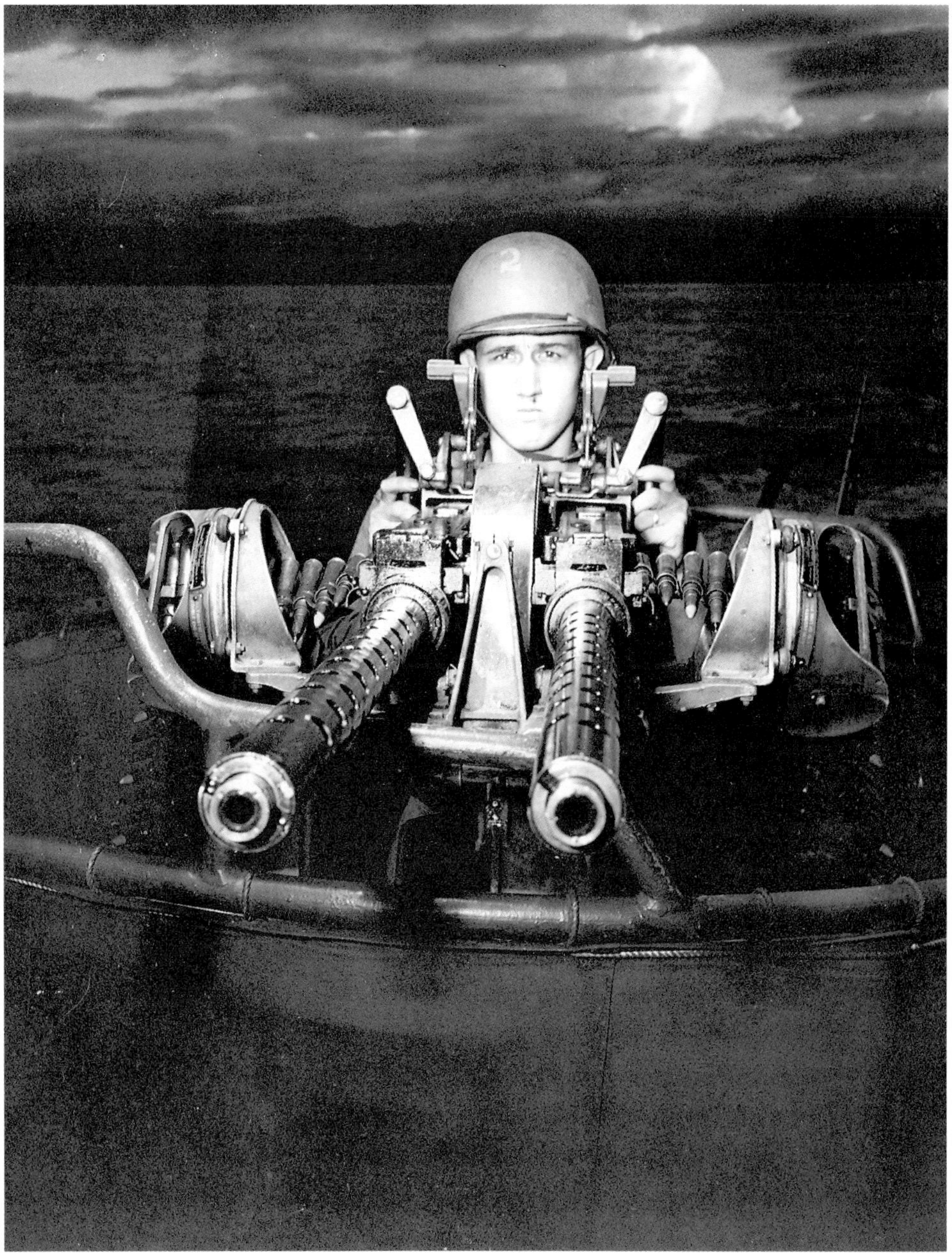

A naval gunner mans his "twin fifty" on board a PT boat off New Guinea. Such craft, well suited to intercepting Japanese coastal reinforcement and supply convoys, were generally armed with four 18 or 21-in torpedoes as well as a varied but light gun armament that often included twin 0·5-in heavy machine guns.

Opposite Top: Men of one of the two marine divisions involved in the invasion of western New Britain push a Jeep ashore onto Cape Gloucester on December 26, 1943. The amphibious vessels are tank landing ships. Their availability in swelling numbers allowed the planning of more, and larger, operations in which heavier vehicles and other equipment could be used.

Opposite Below: Marines wade ashore onto Cape Gloucester from a landing craft manned by personnel of the U.S. Coast Guard. The waterproofed tractor is towing an antitank gun, used for bunker-busting, not for the destruction of tanks, of which the Japanese operated only small numbers.

the operations of the reconnaissance aircraft that provided essential tactical information and probed into enemy areas in search of the next targets. Their use made the development of the type of rolling offensive adopted by MacArthur for the New Guinea campaign much easier.

First Landings on New Britain

As the Australians were sealing off the Huon peninsula with American support, MacArthur launched the 6th Army against New Britain. On December 15, 1943, part of the 1st Cavalry Division (actually an infantry formation that retained its pre-war designation) landed at Arawe on the southern side of New Britain and developed a base area on the Arawe peninsula. Then, on December 26, 1943, the 1st Marine Division of Vice Admiral Kinkaid's 7th Amphibious Force took Long Island on the northern side of the Vitiaz Strait and landed on Cape Gloucester at the extreme western end of New Britain. After four days of hard fighting, the 1st Marine Division had

204

secured a useful area from which they could develop further operations.

Creation of Halsey's 3rd Fleet

Before the Solomons stage of the "Cartwheel" program could begin, Halsey had to turn his SPA forces into the SWPA's 3rd Fleet. This process of reorganization and reinforcement included the creation of the 3rd Amphibious Force under Turner, who was succeeded by Rear Admiral Theodore S. Wilkinson in July. The start of Halsey's part of "Cartwheel" was planned for mid-1943, and MacArthur conceived that it would be completed in a single jump from Guadalcanal to Bougainville. As a preliminary move, Halsey used part of his 43rd Infantry Division to take the Russell Islands, just west of Guadalcanal, on February 11, 1943. This was Operation "Cleanslate," and gave Halsey two more airfields. Halsey now advised MacArthur that, in his opinion, the assault on Bougainville needed more land-based air support than units operating from bases on Guadalcanal and the Russells could furnish.

Revised Plan for the Solomons Campaign

MacArthur was impressed by the logic of Halsey's argument and revised the plan. This eastern component of "Cartwheel" would now involve the capture of a number of intermediate islands that offered airfields. Thus the 3rd Fleet's forces would move along the southern chain of the Solomons to the New Georgia group, where there were three airfields. They would then undertake a direct descent on Bougainville, after diversionary landings had been made on Choiseul Island and the Treasury Islands, which lie between the New Georgia group and Bougainville. On Bougainville and Buka Island, just to

Bougainville
For further references see pages
65, 66, 67, 68, 69, 71, 72, 79, 88

The medium bombers of the 5th Army Air Force proved decisive in the American effort to isolate Japanese garrisons by eliminating the shipping on which they relied for reinforcement and resupply. Here North American B-25 Mitchell bombers sweep over the harbor of Rabaul in a low-level raid directed at shore installations as well as shipping.

its northwest, there were seven airfields which would be invaluable in isolating the Japanese base area on New Britain and New Ireland from reinforcement and resupply by air and sea.

Even though the first six months of 1943 saw little in the way of land operations in the Solomons, an intense air campaign raged over the islands. Starting in January, this campaign peaked in April as the Japanese used their bases as far northwest as Rabaul to launch raid after raid against Allied forces in the southeastern end of the Solomons. The result was a steady and ultimately catastrophic defeat for the Japanese. They had already lost most of their best naval aircrews, and they now learned the fallacy of using inexperienced crews for long and mainly over-water raids against an enemy who was tactically superior, whose aircraft were considerably more advanced, especially the Grumman F6F Hellcat carrierborne and Lockheed P-38 Lightning land-based fighters.

The Americans also took the air war to Japanese bases from Henderson Field, New Guinea, and aircraft carriers. Yamamoto became increasingly worried about the long-term future of the Japanese naval air arm, and between April 7 and 12, he orchestrated what he hoped would be the decisive battle of the air offensive. Most of the depleted naval air groups were called from their carriers at Truk to operate from bases around Rabaul, but they inflicted only minor injury on the Allies, while they themselves suffered catastrophic losses. Many aircraft were lost trying to get back to Rabaul after being damaged in combat over the southeastern Solomons.

The Death of Yamamoto

The death of Yamamoto on April 18 was a major blow to the Japanese. The Japanese naval code had again been broken, and Halsey learned that the admiral was to make a flying visit to Bougainville, He ordered 16 fighters of the USAAF to intercept the two bombers carrying Yamamoto and his staff and shoot them down. The P-38s achieved this daring feat after a long flight from Henderson Field.

Yamamoto was succeeded as commander-in-chief of the Combined Fleet by Admiral Mineichi Koga, and Japan continued its air campaign in the Solomons until the end of 1943. This action achieved nothing significant except the loss of nearly 3,000 aircraft and their crews.

Operation "Toenails"

The central and northwestern Solomons offensive began with Operation "Toenails" against the New Georgia group. Action began on June 30. Rendova Island was captured quickly so that artillery could be landed to support the

Marines scramble down the boarding nets from their transports to reach the landing craft that will deposit them on the assault beach on Bougainville Island.

Under the watchful eye of a gunner on a PT boat, men of the 3rd Marine division head for their landing beaches around Cape Torokina in the Empress Augusta Bay area of Bougainville Island.

main part of the operation, and New Georgia Island was invaded on July 2.

Supported by naval guns and the artillery on Rendova, Major General John H. Hester's 43rd Infantry Division came ashore near Munda. The jungle fighting was bitter in the extreme. The 43rd Infantry Division was reinforced by the 37th Infantry Division, allowing the re-creation of XIV Corps under Major General Oscar W. Griswold, who assumed overall command of the forces ashore on July 18. The airfield outside Munda was the main Japanese air base in the central Solomons, and, under the command of Major General Noburo Sasaki, the Japanese continued to resist the Allies advance with bitter determination. On July 25, the two divisions on New Georgia Island were joined by the 25th Infantry Division, and, after regrouping his forces, Griswold launched a coordinated assault on the airfield, which was captured on August 5. Japanese resistance on New Georgia ended on August 25.

The Americans bypassed Kolombangara Island with its single airfield and launched an amphibious assault on Vella Lavella Island on August 15. The invasion was launched by a single regimental combat team, and after the Japanese defenders were driven back, an airfield was built. In mid-September, elements of the New Zealand 3rd Division replaced the American forces on Vella Lavella, and they completed the elimination of the Japanese forces on the island. This left Kolombangara isolated, and the Japanese evacuated that island. Operations in the central Solomons ended

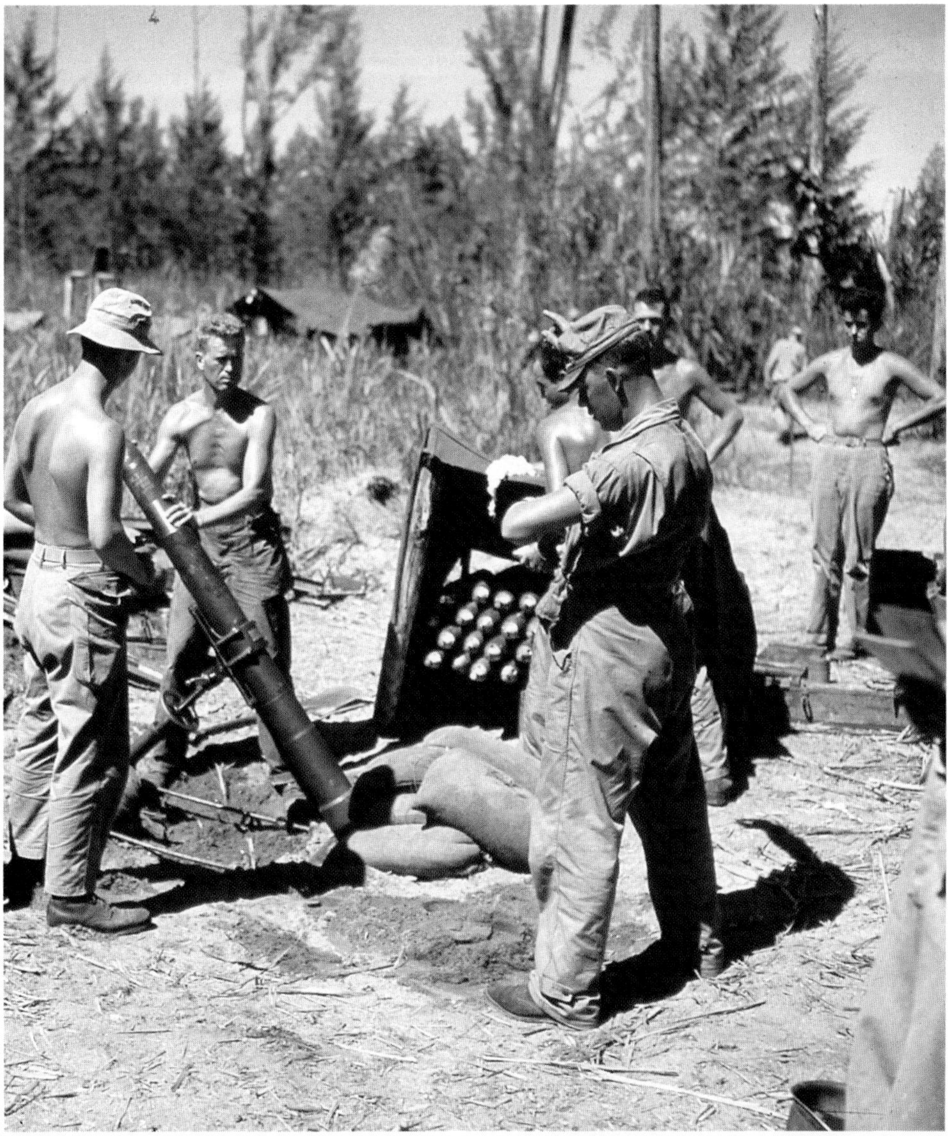

A mortar crew prepares for action on Bougainville Island during April 1944. The crew's commander checks his watch so that his weapon can begin its bombardment of a Japanese position at exactly the right moment.

Below: The landing of the 3rd Marine Division around Cape Torokina met only very sparse Japanese resistance.

on October 7. Allied losses, most of them American, had been 1,136 killed and 4,140 wounded. The 8,000-strong Japanese garrison had lost considerably more, including more than 2,500 dead counted on the battlefield.

Halsey was now ready for the descent on Bougainville. As a diversion, the 2nd Marine Parachute Battalion landed at Voza on the southwestern side of Choiseul on October 27 in Operation "Blissful," but this force was withdrawn on November 3. On the same day that the marines landed on Choiseul, the New Zealand 8th Brigade Group launched Operation "Goodtime" and seized the Treasury Islands as a staging point for the attack on Bougainville.

Left: A 4·2-in mortar team in action near the Laruma River on Bougainville Island during June 6, 1944. By this time, the day of the Allies' D-Day landings in northwestern France against the Germans, the 3rd Marine Division and the 37th Infantry Division had extended the American beach head well inland.

Below: The Japanese were very skillful in creating bunkers and strongpoints. The terrain in such areas often made it impossible to use heavy bunker-busting weapons such as tanks and artillery, so the Americans used the flamethrower as a primary weapon.

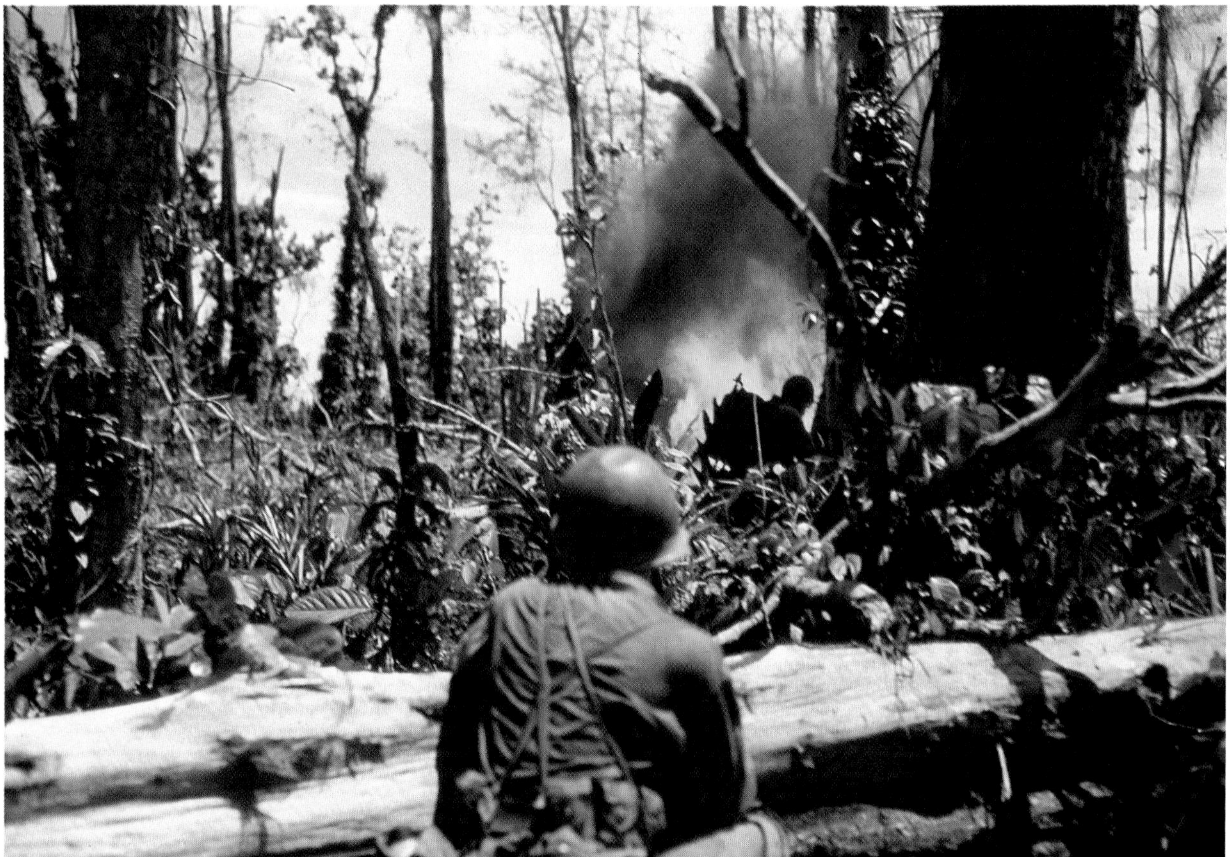

Right: The U.S. maintained a major presence in their enclave on Bougainville until the end of the war, but they were content just to harass the Japanese occupying the bulk of the island. Taken in April 1945, this photograph shows the dug-in positions of the 93rd Infantry Division on the feature known as Hill 260.

Far Right: For the first time, the men of the 3rd Marine Division on Bougainville Island used specially trained dogs as scouts on patrols.

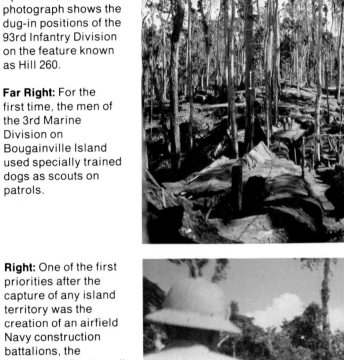

Right: One of the first priorities after the capture of any island territory was the creation of an airfield Navy construction battalions, the legendary "Seabees," acquired a fully justified reputation in this difficult but essential task. They are seen here laying steel matting to create Torokina airfield on Bougainville Island during December 1943.

Opposite Top: Marines on Bougainville Island cautiously examine the body of a Japanese soldier who died with a grenade in his hand.

Opposite Below: Bougainville had its share of dismal weather and bad terrain. Here marines plow their way through deep mud on a trail through the tropical undergrowth.

Below: Airfield construction by the "Seabees" often started even before the fighting had ended. This is Torokina airfield on Bougainville Island during December 1943, with men of the 3rd Marine Division manning a 75-mm pack howitzer to drive back any Japanese attack toward the airfield.

Operation "Cherryblossom"

The invasion of Bougainville, codenamed Operation "Cherryblossom," began on November 1. Commanded by Major General Allen H. Turnage, the 3rd Marine Division of Lieutenant General Vandegrift's I Marine Amphibious Corps landed on each side of Cape Torokina in Empress Augusta Bay. At first, only negligible opposition was encountered from the Japanese 23rd Infantry Regiment. The 37th Infantry Division landed on the 3rd Marine Division's left, and the forces ashore were put under the command of XIV Corps. By the end of the year, XIV Corps had a lodgement ten miles wide and five miles deep, including three airstrips. Empress Augusta Bay had also become a major naval base.

The Naval Battles of the Solomons Campaign

The land operations are only half the story of the war in the central and northern Solomons during the second half of 1943. The other half involved the continuing naval battles between Allied and Japanese maritime forces in the waters around and between these islands.

The Battle of Kula Gulf

The first episode of the campaign was the Battle of Kula Gulf, fought on July 5/6 as the Japanese tried to reinforce their garrison on New Georgia Island with soldiers carried in seven destroyers escorted by three other destroyers. Commanded by Rear Admiral T. Akiyama, this force was intercepted by Rear Admiral W. L. Ainsworth's TG36.1 (three light cruisers and four destroyers). Despite the fact that they had the tactical initiative, radar, larger-caliber guns, and superior armor protection, the Americans suffered a reverse. The Japanese used their better night-fighting tactics and torpedoes to sink the cruiser U.S.S. *Helena*, while losing two destroyers (one sunk, and the other run aground and destroyed later).

The Battles of Kolombangara and Vella Gulf

The next engagement, the Battle of Kolombangara, took place in almost the same waters on July 12/13. Ainsworth's force of three light cruisers (one of them a ship of the Royal New Zealand Navy) and ten destroyers met Rear Admiral S. Izaki's force of one light cruiser and five destroyers escorting four destroyer transports. Again, the Japanese showed their mastery of naval warfare at night, damaging all three American cruisers and sinking one destroyer for the loss of their own cruiser, the *Jintsu*.

The Battle of Vella Gulf was fought on August 6/7 and reversed the trend. A force of six American destroyers encountered four Japanese destroyers and sank three of them without loss to themselves.

The Battle of Vella Lavella

The Battle of Vella Lavella was fought on October 6/7 in waters slightly farther to the northwest, as the Japanese tried to evacuate their surviving 600 men on Vella Lavella. The small evacuation vessels, escorted by Rear Admiral M. Ijuin's nine destroyers, were met by six American destroyers commanded by Captain Frank R. Walker. The result was the last Japanese victory of the Solomons naval campaign. The Japanese caused the loss of one destroyer and seriously damaged two others for the loss of only one of their own number. However, the threat of American reinforcements forced Ijuin to call off the evacuation attempt.

By this stage of the Solomons campaign, American air power was only marginally challenged by the Japanese. A pilot of VF-17 describes a successful air combat to a comrade.

The Battle of Empress Augusta Bay

The last naval engagement of the campaign was the Battle of Empress Augusta Bay, which took place on November 2. In an effort to reach and destroy the American invasion fleet off Bougainville, the Japanese sent in Vice Admiral Sentaro Omori with two heavy cruisers, two light cruisers, and six destroyers. This force was intercepted by Rear Admiral A. Stanton Merrill's TF39, consisting of four light cruisers and eight destroyers. Merrill opted to use radar-controlled gunfire and positioned his ships to fire on the front and flank of the Japanese ships. The Allies suffered heavy damage to only one destroyer, but sank the light cruiser *Sendai* and one destroyer, and damaged most of the other Japanese ships.

These engagements were fought on a smaller scale than the earlier battles of the Guadalcanal campaign, but the Allies had clearly digested the implications of the earlier fighting. They quickly developed tactical superiority over the Japanese, with radar playing a major part in winning night encounters.

The last naval battles connected with the Solomons campaign resulted from Koga's decision to reinforce Japan's 8th Fleet, based at Rabaul, for an attack on the Allied forces off Bougainville. Kogo sent seven heavy cruisers, one light cruiser, and four destroyers from Truk under the command of Vice Admiral Takeo Kurita. When Halsey learned that the Japanese ships' had left Truk, the only strike force available to the 3rd Fleet was Rear Admiral Frederick C. Sherman's TF38, consisting of the fleet carrier *Saratoga* and the light carrier U.S.S. *Princeton* plus escorts. On November 5, Sherman's aircraft attacked the

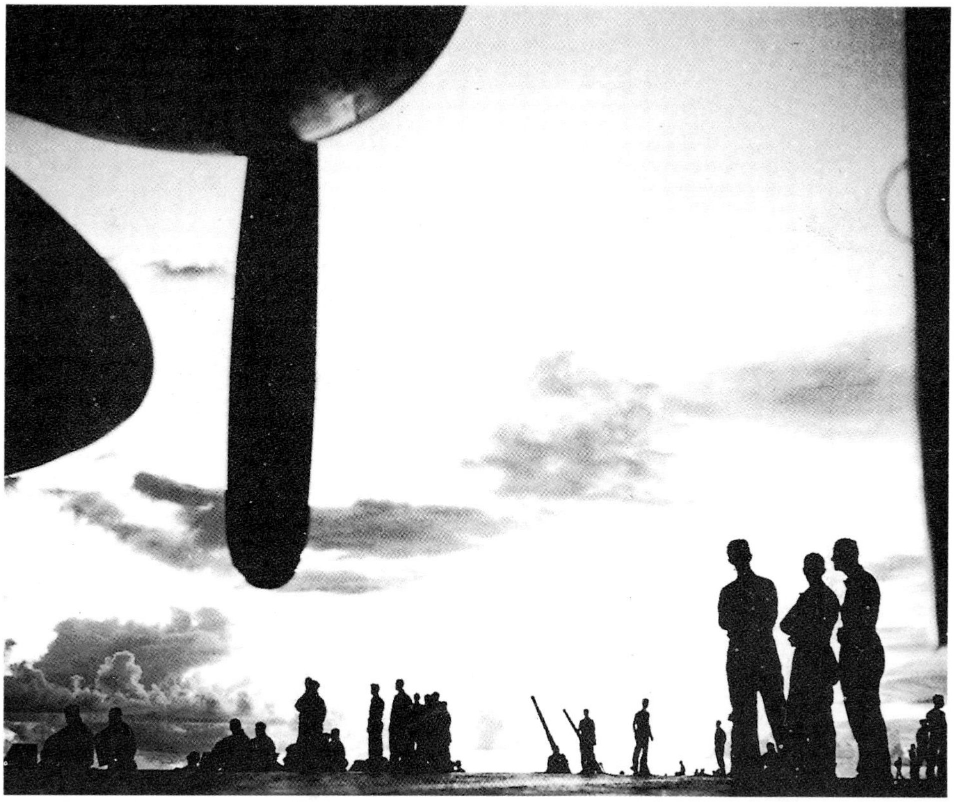

Dawn over the flight deck of the fleet carrier *Saratoga* before a raid on Rabaul in November 1943.

Japanese forces in Rabaul, badly damaging six cruisers and destroyers. Kurita was forced to call off his attack. On November 11, a repeat raid was mounted against the Japanese ships in Rabaul by aircraft from Rear Admiral Alfred E. Montgomery's TG50.3, which included the fleet carriers U.S.S. *Bunker Hill* and U.S.S. *Essex*, and the light carrier U.S.S. *Independence*. The Japanese were ready for such an attack, and the 183 American aircraft received a hostile reception. Even so, more damage was caused to the Japanese ships, and after a Japanese air attack on TG50.3 had been beaten off, Kurita pulled his ships back to Truk.

Rabaul Now To Be Isolated and Bypassed

Meanwhile, the JCS had decided that the Japanese base area on New Britain and New Ireland was not capable of mounting any significant offensive action. MacArthur was instructed to isolate and bypass the area. Otherwise, men and equipment would be wasted in an attack that had no real value, but which would of course be defended tenaciously by the Japanese.

When it approved "Cartwheel" in March 1943, the joint chiefs had in essence approved MacArthur's plan to push back toward the Philippines via New Guinea and the eastern end of the East Indies. The JCS also felt, however, that a Central Pacific offensive was important. At the "Trident" Conference in Washington in May 1943, the JCS therefore proposed an overall Pacific scheme that was approved by the American and British Combined Chiefs of Staff committee.

In basic terms (and including both British and Chinese efforts on the Asian mainland) this strategic plan called for the seizure of a foothold in Asia near Hong Kong. This location would then be developed into the main base from which Japan could be attacked and possibly invaded. American forces would reach this area by opening up the Celebes Sea and retaking part of the Philippines. Within this overall concept, the joint chiefs decided that Nimitz's forces should make the main westward move, aided by a subsidiary thrust through New Guinea by MacArthur's SWPA.

MacArthur disputed the validity of this

plan for months. He was sure that an offensive through the Pacific would be too long, secure no important strategic objectives, involve costly invasions of island bastions, and not provide the benefits of land-based air power. MacArthur therefore argued that the main thrust should be made through New Guinea by his SWPA.

The JCS decided firmly in favor of the Pacific Ocean Area offensive under Nimitz. This plan would be easier to support in logistic terms, could take full advantage of the mobility offered by American naval power, would encounter fewer terrain and disease problems, and would strike at the eastern sector of Japan's defensive perimeter, which was thought to be weaker than the southeastern sector. In October, the JCS added another reason, the Mariana Islands were needed as a base from which the USAAF's new strategic bomber, the Boeing B-29 Superfortress, could devastate Japan.

POA and SWPA Meet in the Philippines

Thus the stage was set for a two-prong advance to the Philippines, where the forces of the SWPA and POA met on October 20, 1944.

As this strategic concept was being finalized, the Japanese were reluctantly revising their own overall defensive plan. Allied naval and air power were decimating Japanese merchant shipping and air power, so the Japanese decided to pull back their defensive perimeter. The new border was a shorter and more easily defended line running in a huge arc from the Kurile Islands to Burma via the Bonin Islands, Mariana Islands. Caroline Islands, western New Guinea, and the East Indies. Outposts forward of this main perimeter would trade space for time as the new line was being established, and the defense of the new line would buy time for Japan to rebuild her offensive capability.

One of the underlying factors that forced the Japanese to contract was the loss of their outposts on the Aleutian islands of Attu and Kiska in August 1943. At the beginning of that year, these islands, supported by the ships of Vice Admiral Hosogaya's Northern Area Force and by air bases on Paramushiro Island in the northern Kuriles, looked secure. Allied strength in the area was centered on Dutch Harbor in the central Aleutians.

Japanese Defeat in the Aleutians

On March 26, 1943, Rear Admiral Charles H. McMorris was cruising west of Attu with TG16.6 (one heavy cruiser, one light cruiser, and four destroyers) when he encountered a more powerful Japanese force of two heavy cruisers, two light cruisers, and four destroyers escorting three large transports ferrying reinforcements to Attu. The result was the Battle of the Komandorski Islands, in essence an old-fashioned gun duel at long range.

The fire of the Japanese ships crippled the heavy cruiser U.S.S. *Salt Lake City*, while the American guns severely damaged the heavy cruiser *Nachi*. The Japanese had a huge advantage, but as Hosogaya closed the range to smother the American ships with shorter-range fire, three of the American destroyers drove forward in a desperate torpedo attack. Hosogaya broke away and then, fearing that American bombers would have been called in from Dutch Harbor, he broke off the action and returned to the Kuriles. From then on, reinforcements and supplies for the Japanese forces on Attu and Kiska had to be delivered by submarine.

The U.S. now thought the time was ripe to eliminate the Japanese garrisons from the two islands. On May 11, Rear Admiral Francis W. Rockwell's amphibious force began landing 12,000 men of the 7th Infantry Division on Attu, which was held by 2,500 Japanese. The fighting lasted 18 days as the Americans drew the defenders out of their complex of defensive positions. The operation was completed on May 29. The 7th Infantry Division had suffered 561 killed and 1,136 wounded. With the exception of 29 men who surrendered, the Japanese garrison was wiped out.

With Attu back in American hands,

An altogether harsher climate was found in the Aleutian Islands which run from Alaska toward Siberia. These are men of the combined American and Canadian force that landed on Kiska during August 15, 1943, only to learn that the Japanese had evacuated their garrison.

Among the items abandoned by the Japanese when they evacuated Kiska were these three midget submarines, deliberately wrecked by internal explosions. The boats were each designed to carry two 18-in torpedoes in superimposed bow tubes.

Kiska, which was closer to the mainland along the Aleutian chain, was isolated, and the Japanese decided to evacuate the 5,185-man garrison. In the first attempt, on May 26, seven out of 13 submarines were lost, and the Japanese therefore decided to use surface ships. Skillfully using fog and darkness, two cruisers and six destroyers evacuated the entire garrison on July 28/29.

The operation was not detected by the NPA, and on August 15, a 35,000-man American and Canadian force began landing on Kiska. After a two-day sweep that captured nothing but four abandoned dogs, the landing force was sure that the Japanese had gone.

Buildup in the Central Pacific Area

This sideshow in the Aleutians did not materially affect development in the CPA. Between January and October 1943, vast numbers of men, aircraft, and ships began to assemble in the Hawaiian, Fijian, and New Hebrides Islands as

Nimitz concentrated the strength for his westward drive. The core of this offensive force was Vice Admiral Spruance's 5th Fleet, which by October mustered eight aircraft carriers, seven battleships, seven heavy cruisers, three light cruisers, and 34 destroyers. Providing amphibious assault capability was Turner's 5th Amphibious Force, which was capable of moving and landing the 100,000 men of Major General Holland M. "Howling Mad" Smith's V Amphibious Corps, together with all its supplies and equipment. Additional offensive capability was provided by the land-based aircraft of Major General Willis A. Hale's 7th AAF, based in the Ellice Islands.

Another key element of the plan was a new type of vehicle, the LVT (Landing Vehicle Tracked), which had been developed to replace conventional landing craft. Experience had shown that passages through the reefs were always targeted by Japanese guns, and the landing craft often had to drop their assault troops in comparatively deep water, forcing the soldiers to wade ashore under intense Japanese fire. Developed as an amphibious load carrier, the LVT was propelled by its tracks. It could crawl over reefs and right up onto the beach. The early vehicles were lightly armored, and in the campaign, they proved both vulnerable and invaluable. The craft was extensively redeveloped for the rest of the war, and its greater payload, protection, and offensive firepower made it a truly war-winning weapon in the American arsenal.

Capture of the Marshalls

Nimitz's first objective was the Marshall Islands, but he was unable to secure enough land forces for so difficult a target and substituted the less well-protected Gilbert Islands. This group lies about 600 miles southeast of the Marshalls and became a feasible target when one of the SWPA's marine divisions was reallocated to the POA. Nimitz's planners knew that the Japanese defenses were centered on the Tarawa and Makin atolls, two strings of low, coral-reef islets clustered around a central lagoon.

The planners also knew that despite their small size, the islets would be

One of the most important weapons in the U.S. arsenal for amphibious operations was the Landing Vehicle, Tracked. This was developed in a number of forms, here represented by the initial LVT 1. Powered by a 146-hp Hercules gasoline engine, it drove cleated tracks at a land speed of 15 mph and a water speed of 4 knots. Land and water ranges were 75 and 50 miles respectively. The LVT 1 was 21 ft 6 in long and 9 ft 10 in wide, and weighed 19,600 lb. The crew was three, and the load-carrying capability amounted to 20 men or 4,500 pounds of cargo.

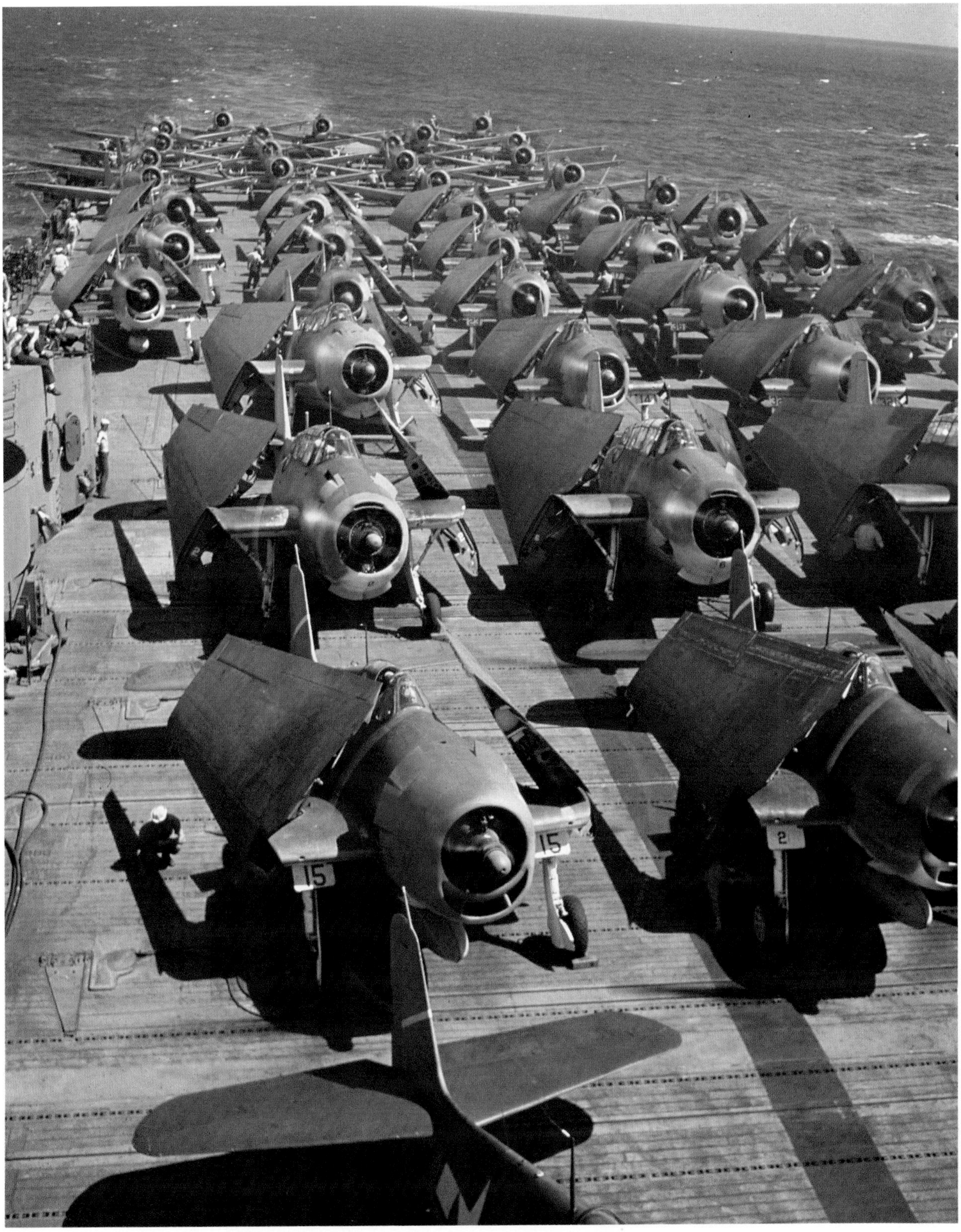

A view aft from the island superstructure of the fleet carrier *Yorktown* during the American offensive to recapture the Gilbert Islands in November 1943. The aircraft are Grumman F6F Hellcats, the type of fighter that snatched air superiority away from the Mitsubishi A6M Zero through a combination of technical excellence and numerical superiority.

Pilots receive a last-minute briefing in one of the "ready rooms" of the fleet carrier *Lexington*. Tactical intelligence was sometimes faulty, and the execution of plans based on it was sometimes marred by mistakes, but the U.S. Navy's operational and strategic intelligence was generally excellent.

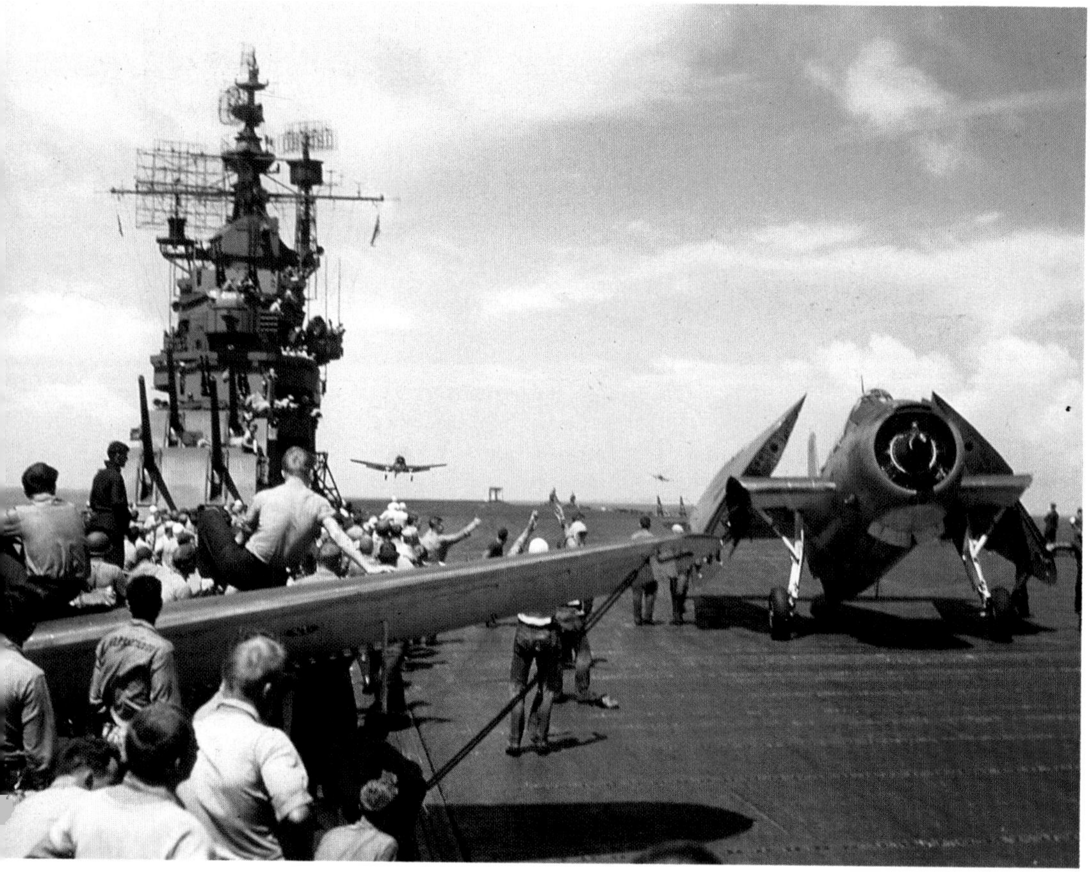

Grumman F6F Hellcat fighters return to the fleet carrier *Lexington* after operations during the capture of the Gilbert Islands during November 1943. This was the first of the U.S. Navy-commanded "island hopping" campaigns of the war, and many valuable lessons were learned.

A pattern of smoke rings forms in front of the gun muzzles as an American cruiser uses its secondary battery to blast the Japanese on Makin Atoll in the Gilbert Islands before the landing of November 20, 1943.

difficult to take. They also feared intervention by the Japanese Combined Fleet from its main base at Truk. The Combined Fleet had lost most of its carriers in 1942, and some of its battleships and heavy cruisers in 1943, but it still possessed formidable strength. Its surface warships could wreak total havoc if they got in among an invasion force. Fortunately, the Japanese were preoccupied with events on Bougainville, and the Combined Fleet stayed at Truk.

Before the POA committed its amphibious forces to their invasion beaches in the Gilberts, the islands were thoroughly pasted by air bombardment and naval gunfire. This pre-invasion campaign started on November 13 and lasted until November 17 in the case of the bombers and November 20 in the case of the warships. It seemed that nothing and no one could survive such a mass of high explosive, but events soon proved this feeling wrong.

On November 20, the reinforced 165th Infantry Regiment of Major General Ralph C. Smith's 27th Infantry Division landed on Makin, where the Japanese garrison included 250 naval combat troops and 550 Korean labor troops. The Allies sent overwhelming force in against the Japanese, but it still took four days of hard fighting to win Makin. The Allied casualties were 66 killed and 152 wounded. All the defenders were killed with the exception of one naval soldier and 104 laborers who surrendered.

The four days of the Makin battle gave the Japanese time to intervene with submarines, one of which torpedoed and sank the escort carrier U.S.S. *Liscombe Bay*, with 640 officers and men on board.

Bloody Tarawa

Makin was a tough nut to crack. Tarawa was much harder. The Japanese bastion islet was Betio, whose 300 flat and sandy acres were covered with thick vegetation except around the airstrip. Commanded

Right: Grumman TBF Avenger carrierborne bombers on their way to attack Japanese positions appear to be shepherding the landing craft carrying infantry for the invasion of Makin.

Opposite Top: Men of the 2nd Marine Division shelter under the palm log beach defenses of Betio, the main Japanese position in the Tarawa Atoll of the Gilbert Islands. Much of the Japanese defensive complex survived the pre-landing air and sea bombardment.

Opposite Below: Marines top one of the "high points" on Betio, a tiny piece of land captured by the U.S. Marine Corps at the expense of one of the heaviest casualty rates ever suffered in American military history.

Below: American aircraft strafe a small Japanese freighter off the Marshall Islands on January 16, 1944.

by Rear Admiral Keiji Shibasaki, the 4,700-man garrison included 2,620 combat veterans and more than 2,000 labor troops. They manned a defense complex of underground bunkers, concealed shelters, 400 concrete pillboxes, seven light tanks, and 25 pieces of artillery. More than 20 coast-defense guns ranging in caliber from 80-mm weapons to 8-inch guns brought in from Singapore, were ranged inland from beaches full of mines and festooned with barbed wire.

Launched on November 20, Operation "Galvanic" called for an assault on the inner, or lagoon, side of the island. But, as the men of Major General Julian C. Smith's 2nd Marine Division found to their cost, pre-war maps and inadequate wartime reconnaissance did not show the inner set of reefs that stalled the landing craft hundreds of yards from shore. The men of the 2nd and 8th Marine Regiments suffered terrible casualties as they waded ashore. As they reached the beach, the Allied naval bombardment lifted. This meant that the marines would not be hit by their own gunfire, but it left them stranded on the shore. They had little chance of driving inland against a Japanese garrison that seemed

Aftermath of the battle: bodies, wrecked vehicles, and other debris litter Betio's very fringes. Much of the heaviest fighting took place on the edges as the marines tried to claw their way onto the islet.

to have suffered no significant losses from the pre-invasion air and naval bombardments.

By nightfall, about 1,500 of the 5,000 U.S. marines landed had been killed or wounded. During the night, tanks, guns, and ammunition were landed, and the following day the divisional reserve suffered 344 casualties as they landed. With the aid of spotters on the shore, naval gunfire resumed, and close air support was called in as the marines inched inland. There was no room to maneuver, so costly frontal attacks were the only tactics that could be used.

With the exception of a pocket on the northwestern side of the islet, the Japanese were driven back toward the eastern end of the island beyond the edge of the airstrip. Most of the force was killed in a suicidal attack during the night of November 22/23, and the northwestern pocket was finally crushed in the early afternoon of November 23.

The marines suffered just over 1,000 men killed and 2,072 wounded, while navy corpsmen suffered more than 120 casualties. All of the 4,700-man Japanese garrison was killed, except for about 100 men, only 17 of them soldiers, who were taken prisoner.

The Clearance of the Gilberts

Of the other islets in the Tarawa Atoll, Bairiki, Buarika, and Naa were taken on November 21, 27, and 28 respectively. Operation "Galvanic" had succeeded in taking territory, but, the ratio between troops engaged and casualties make it one of the costliest battles in American military history. However, it had also taught the Allies many invaluable lessons about Japanese defensive methods. The tactics needed to defeat the Japanese were used in the ladder of islands stretching westward to the Philippines, which reduced casualties in later island battles. In the short term, the capture of the Gilberts opened land bases for aircraft to be used in the attack on the Marshalls.

This step was divided into two stages, codenamed Operations "Flintlock" and "Catchpole." As a preliminary, Vice Admiral Marc A. Mitcher's Fast Carrier Task Force (six fleet carriers and six light carriers escorted by fast battleships, cruisers, and destroyers) moved forward in four groups to destroy Japanese air strength in the Marshalls, paving the way for Spruance's 5th Fleet, whose assault formation was Turner's 5th Amphibious Force with the one army and two marine divisions of H. M. Smith's V Amphibious Corps. This force had thoroughly digested the implications of the fight for Tarawa and was now a more effective formation.

The Capture of Kwajalein

"Flintlock" was designed to secure the citadel area of the Marshalls, the atoll of Kwajalein. The Japanese garrison of 8,500 men under Rear Admiral M. Akiyama was deployed mainly in the south on Kwajalein Islet and in the north on Roi and Namur islets. These three were to be assaulted simultaneously by Major General Charles H. Corlett's 7th Infantry Division and Major General Harry Schmidt's 4th Marine Division.

The 5th Fleet staged through Majuro Atoll, which was taken on January 30, 1944, and descended on Kwajalein on February 1. The 32nd and 184th Infantry Regiments landed on Kwajalein while smaller detachments took the smaller islets of Ninni, Enubuj, and Loi. The 23rd and 24th Marine Regiments landed on Roi and Namur, while smaller detachments took the adjacent islets.

As on Tarawa, the fighting was severe, but this time the Allies had the right tactics. Roi and Namur had been taken by February 2, and the last resistance in Kwajalein ended on February 4. The whole operation involved the landing of 41,000 American troops, of whom 486

Douglas SBD Dauntless dive-bombers fill the flight deck of the fleet carrier *Lexington* after returning from a mission providing close support for the marines on Tarawa.

Douglas SBD Dauntles dive-bombers attack the Japanese radio direction-finding station on Ulalu, an island of the Truk group where the Combined Fleet had its southern operating base.

were killed and 1,295 wounded. The Japanese lost the whole garrison except for 130 men taken prisoner.

Triumph of Air Power at Truk

"Catchpole" was designed to take Eniwetok Atoll at the northwestern tip of the Marshalls. The Allied commanders had been surprised by the Combined Fleet's lack of response to "Flintlock," but Koga felt that his lack of carriers ruled out any attack on the American force in the Marshalls. Spruance wanted to guarantee that "Catchpole" was equally unhindered by Japan's still powerful force of surface warships. On February 17 and 18, he sent the FCTF, otherwise known as TF58, to attack Truk. Mitscher's carriers achieved surprise, and though Koga managed to save most of his warships, Allied carrierborne aircraft found 50 merchant ships in Truk's lagoon and 365 aircraft on its Truk's airstrips. By noon, American aircraft had sunk 200,000 tons of merchant shipping and destroyed 275 Japanese aircraft. Spruance was meanwhile combing the area with one battleship, four heavy cruisers, and four destroyers, which sank one light cruiser and one destroyer. Koga saw that Truk was now hopelessly vulnerable and withdrew the Combined Fleet to the Philippine Sea, behind the barrier of the Carolines and Marianas. With the Combined Fleet gone, Truk was no longer a significant target for the Allies, who decided to bypass this once great base and leave it to "wither on the vine" as they moved forward to attack more important targets.

Reduction of Eniwetok

"Catchpole" began on February 17 with Brigadier General Thomas Watson's 8,000-man Tactical Group 1 attacking the Japanese garrison. Its 3,400 men were from Major General Yoshima Nishida's veteran 1st Amphibious Brigade, which held Eniwetok and Parry islets on the atoll's southern side, and Engebi Islet

Above: American carrierborne aircraft attack Japanese shipping off Dublon, another island of the Truk group. This raid, undertaken in April 1944, was just one of a sequence that steadily reduced the ability of the Japanese to operate effectively out of Truk.

Right: Men of the 4th Marine Division land from their LVT amphibious tractor during the assault on Namur during February 1, 1944. Namur was one of two islets attacked at the northern end of Kwajalein Atoll during Operation "Flintlock."

Top: A dead Japanese lies just in front of two men of the 22nd Marine Regiment.

Center: Devastation on Kwajalein after the Americans had mopped up the atoll's last Japanese defenders.

Bottom: Japanese dead litter a trench on Namur islet.

Above: The capture of Eniwetok islet, the main Japanese position in the atoll of the same name, was entrusted to two battalions of the 106th Infantry Regiment and one battalion of the 22nd Marine Division. This is a flamethrower team of the 22nd Marines.

Left: Men of the U.S. Marine Corps and members of the U.S. Coast Guard who crewed their assault craft join in displaying a Japanese battle flag captured on Engebi islet. This northernmost part of Eniwetok Atoll was taken by two battalions of the 22nd Marine Regiment.

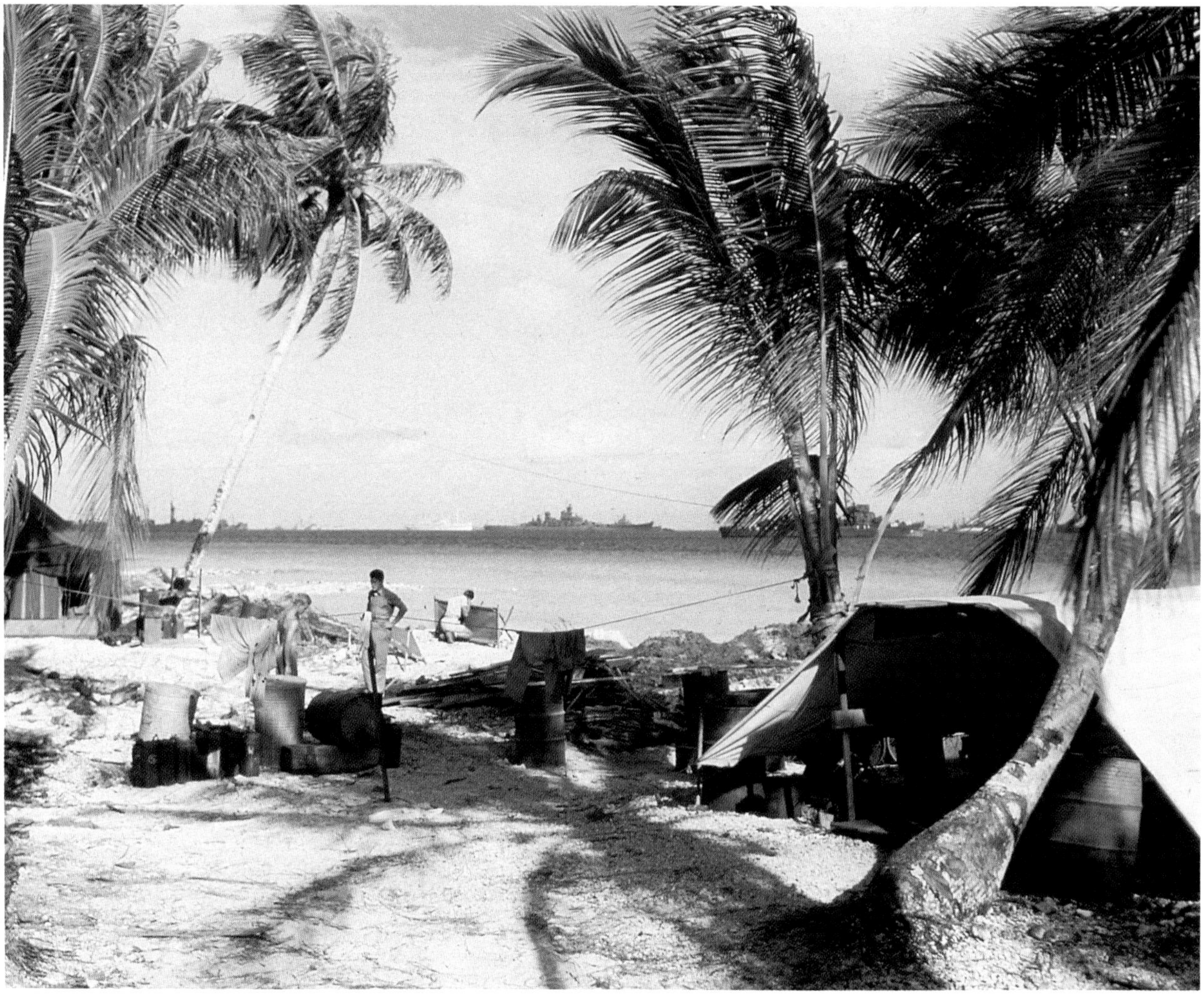

As the American advance surged toward Japan through the Pacific, early conquests became base areas where fleet anchorages and rest camps were established. Seen in 1945, this facility is at Kwajalein Atoll in the Marshall Islands.

(with the atoll's only airstrip) on the northern side.

Engebi was attacked by two battalions of the 22nd Marine Regiment and overrun by February 19. Eniwetok was attacked on February 19 by two battalions of the 106th Infantry Regiment and one battalion of the 22nd Marine Regiment and overrun by February 21. Parry was attacked on February 22 by three battalions of the 22nd Marine Regiment and overrun by February 23. American casualties in "Catchpole" were 348 killed and 866 wounded, while the Japanese had lost virtually the entire garrison except for a few labor troops who surrendered.

Once Kawajalein and Eniwetok were in American hands, many thousands more Japanese troops in the Marshalls were cut off. Since they had no way to interfere with the next Allied moves, they were left in passive isolation for the rest of the war.

The Isolation of Rabaul Continues

As these events were unfolding in the POA, the SWPA was closing its net around Rabaul. Between January and May 1943, the land forces of Halsey's 3rd Fleet were involved in a comparatively small but bitter campaign in the Solomons to contain and wear down the Japanese 17th Army. The main Japanese strength was on Bougainville, where the Japanese launched numerous attacks to try to destroy the Allied lodgement around Empress Augusta Bay. The uncoordinated attacks were driven back with high Japanese losses. By May, the Japanese were starving and near despair, and the scale and intensity of the attacks declined dramatically.

On February 15, the New Zealand 3rd Division seized Green Island as the site for a new air base from which Rabaul could be attacked. The net finally closed in on Rabaul after two more landings.

On February 29, the SWPA's 1st Cavalry Division landed a large reconnaissance force on Los Negros Island in the Admiralty Islands northwest of Rabaul. It soon developed into a full-scale invasion, which cleared Los Negros and the larger Manus Island by March 23. American losses were 326 killed and 1,189 wounded, while Japanese losses were 3,280 dead and 89 prisoners.

On March 20, the 3rd Fleet's 4th Marine Division landed on Emirau Island in the St. Matthias group, northwest of Kavieng. They met no opposition and quickly occupied the island before moving forward to seize the larger Mussau Island. American air bases were quickly built in the Admiralty and St. Matthias groups, effectively cutting Japanese lines of communication to New Britain and New Ireland. With its task in the SWPA completed, Halsey's 3rd Fleet reverted to the command of the POA in June, giving Nimitz two large and combat-hardened fleets to continue operations in the Central Pacific.

The final episode of the isolation of Rabaul was the expansion of the American lodgement at the western end of New Britain. Between January and March 6, the 1st Marine and 40th Infantry Divisions had pushed the edge of the lodgement as far east as the Willaumez Peninsula. They halted in this less disease-ridden area and eventually handed over the containment of the Japanese to the Australians. The New Britain operation cost the Americans 493 killed and 1,402 wounded, while the Japanese casualties included 4,600 killed and 329 taken prisoner.

Coast Hopping on New Guinea

Support for these operations on New Britain, and for the landings in the Admiralty and St. Matthias groups, was provided by the tactical aircraft of the 5th AAF operating from bases in the Saidor area of New Guinea. This area was taken after an Allied landing by a regimental combat team of the 32nd Infantry Division on January 2, 1944. This force came ashore to the northwest of Saidor and soon enveloped the Japanese garrison. On March 23, the Americans linked up with Australians advancing from Finschhafen, and the Japanese garrison of Saidor melted away into the interior of New Guinea.

The Japanese now planned to hold the western end of New Guinea as the cor-

A man of the 4th Marine Division in the jungle of Emirau Island, part of the St. Matthias group northwest of New Ireland. An unopposed landing was made here on March 20, 1944, and helped to complete the isolation of the Japanese base areas in New Britain and New Ireland.

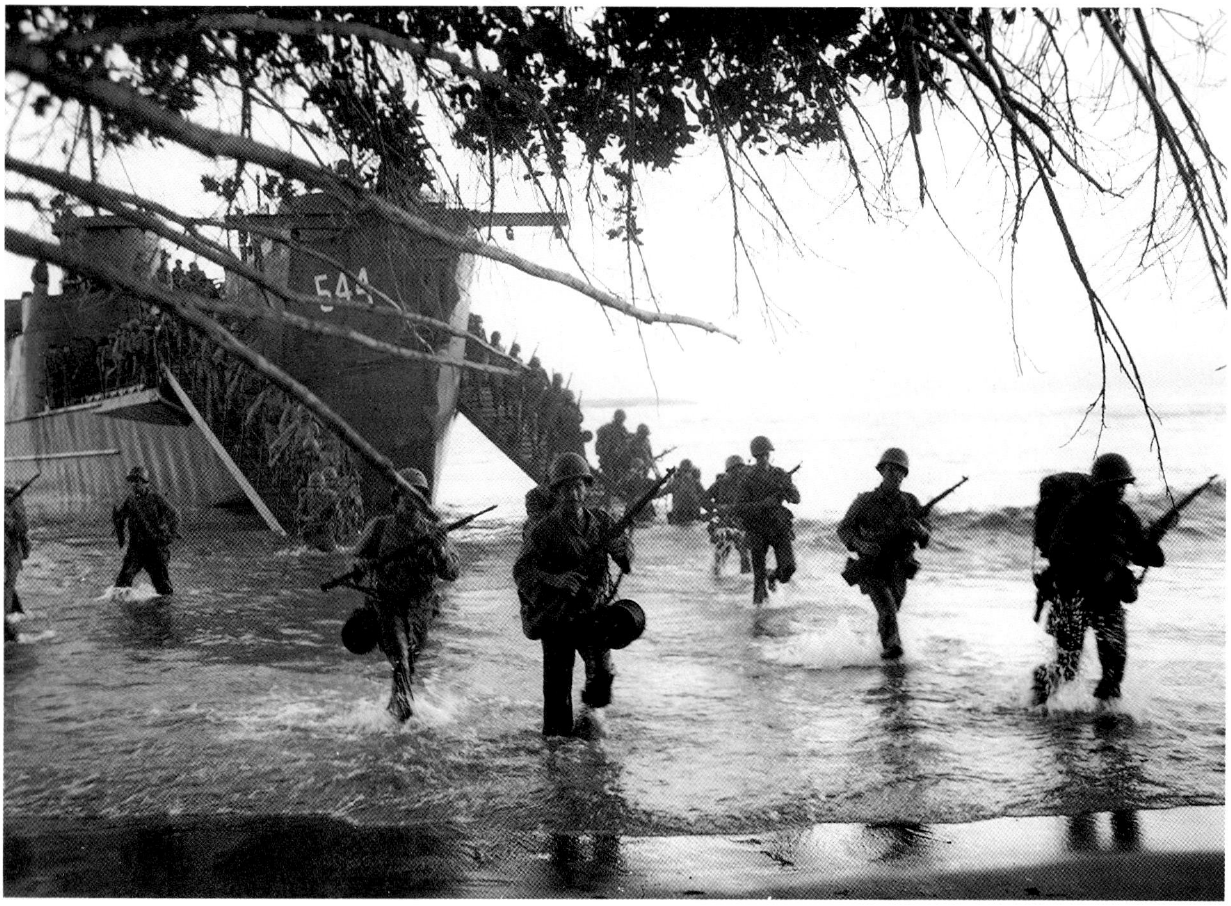

The last American assault landing in New Guinea was made at Sausapor on the northwestern end of this huge island. The landing on July 30, 1944, was unopposed, and MacArthur's forces could now ready themselves for the drive toward the Philippines.

nerstone of the defensive perimeter in this area. Lieutenant General Jo Imamura's Japanese 2nd Area Army therefore established a major base at Hollandia. This area was beyond the reach of the 5th AAF's tactical aircraft, and the Japanese began to build airfields for future offensive and defensive operations. The first airfield was completed on April 3, and Imamura felt sure that MacArthur would not attempt a landing in an area beyond the support of Allied land-based aircraft. Imamura told Lieutenant General Hotaze Adachi to locate only a small part of his 65,000-man Japanese 18th Army in this base area so that the army's main strength could be based farther forward, in the area between Madang and Wewak.

MacArthur's Strategic Masterstroke

MacArthur had in fact decided to bypass these Japanese forward positions and strike directly at Hollandia. As Imamura had surmised, MacArthur was concerned that this would take his forces beyond the range of their own land-based air support, but with the permission of the JCS, he secured from Nimitz the loan of Mitscher's FCTF. Worried about the threat to his carriers from Japanese land-based air power, Nimitz insisted that the FCTF's carriers remain in New Guinea waters for only four days. It was therefore essential for MacArthur to secure a forward air base before the carriers pulled out. His plan called for the simultaneous capture of Hollandia, under cover of the FCTF's aircraft, and Aitape, a forward air base about 125 miles to the southeast, which was within range of Saidor-based aircraft.

The operation began on March 30, when the 5th AAF launched a campaign against the airfield complex around Hollandia. This engagement lasted up to April 19, and at the cost of just a few Allied aircraft, destroyed about 400 aircraft on the ground and another 120 in the air. On April 1, the Australians pushed forward toward Madang, and Adachi was

Troops advance though trees shattered by naval gunfire before the landing on Wake Island on May 17, 1944.

so worried that he called in additional men from Hollandia, further weakening the base area.

The landings at Hollandia and Aitape began on April 22. At Hollandia, the 7th Amphibious Force put the 24th and 41st Infantry Divisions ashore on beaches 25 miles apart, east and west of Hollandia itself. At the same time, two reinforced regiments landed at Aitape.

The capture of Aitape took two days, another bitterly fought battle. Even as the battle was raging, engineers prepared an airfield for operational service, and the first American aircraft landed on April 24 just as the battle was ending. The struggle cost the Americans 450 killed and 2,500 wounded. Japanese dead numbered about 9,000.

At Hollandia, the two assault divisions moved inland against weak resistance with the intention of meeting around the airfield complex located inland behind the coastal mountains. The fighting lasted until April 27. As the carriers withdrew on April 26, land-based aircraft moved in from Aitape. American losses were about 100 killed and 1,000 wounded, while those of the Japanese were about 5,000 dead. Another 5,000 Japanese fled inland to the jungle.

Complete Success in New Guinea

MacArthur's forces now continued their surge to the west. On May 17, an amphibious assault took Wake Island and its airfields. The Americans were disappointed to find that here, as at Hollandia, the earth could not support the weight of long-range heavy bombers. SWPA planners though that Biak Island, which already supported a Japanese airfield, might be more suitable, and on May 27 the 41st Infantry Division landed in an amphibious assault. The division met unexpectedly heavy resistance, and it was June 29 before the island was declared secure. The Americans suffered 2,700 casualties and the Japanese 10,000 or more. Between July 2 and 7, Numfoor

U.S. Marine Corps Raider Bougainville, 1943-44

The kajder units were an elite subdivision of the U.S. Marine Corps used for reconnaissance and assaults on targets that were particularly difficult because of their geographical location. This marine raider wears standard kit for island fighting in the Southwest Pacific. Notable features are the large quantity of ammunition carried for the 0·3-inch (7·62-mm) caliber M1 Garand semiautomatic rifle, which has an ammunition pouch on its butt, and the M2A1 fragmentation grenade in the raider's right hand. The latter had a 4/4·8-second delay fuse, weighed 1·31 pounds (0·595 kg), and measured 4·5 inches (114 mm) in length and 2¼ inches (57 mm diameter.

An American infantryman remains wholly unconcerned by the body of a dead Japanese during the fighting on New Guinea.

Island was taken to provide more airfields, and on July 30 the unoccupied Sausapor, at the western tip of New Guinea, was seized. The New Guinea campaign was over, and MacArthur was poised for the SWPA's leap back to the Philippines.

By this time, the Americans were posing a double threat to the Japanese defensive perimeter. As MacArthur advanced through its southeastern sector, Nimitz was pushing through the east.

At the beginning of April 1944, Koga was killed in an air crash. His successor as commander-in-chief of the Combined Fleet was Admiral Soemu Toyoda, a more forceful leader and Yamamoto's true successor in the belief that the Pacific Fleet must be destroyed. On May 3, Toyoda ordered Vice Admiral Jisaburo Ozawa to trail the bait of his 1st Mobile Fleet, containing Japan's somewhat revived carrier force, as a means of luring the Pacific Fleet into the area bounded by the Palau Islands, Yap Island, and Woleai Island in the eastern Carolines. Then, according to Toyoda's plan, the Allied naval force could be destroyed by a combination of carrierborne and land-based air power, supported by the guns of the 1st Mobile Fleet's five battleships and ten heavy cruisers. The three basic components of

Soemu Toyoda
For further references see pages 98, 107

A PT boat eases along the New Guinea coast, complete with a party of friendly natives.

An American artillery crew prepares to fire an 18-pounder gun borrowed from the Australians on New Guinea.

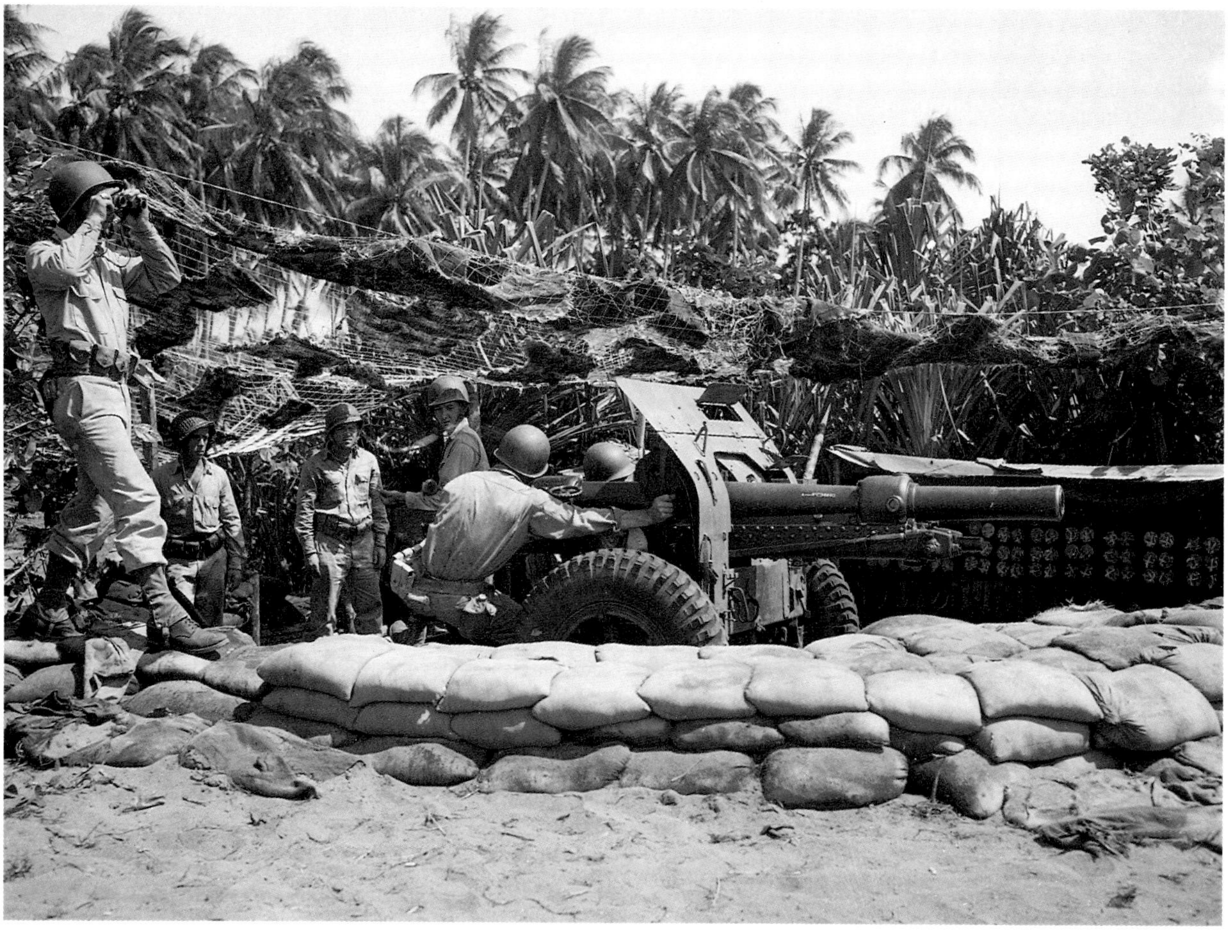

The jungle fighting in New Guinea was similar to combat in the later war in Vietnam. A fire fight began when:

A Japanese advance patrol, usually four or five riflemen and a light machine gun team, picked its way single file through the undergrowth. When they encountered an American patrol, gunfire might be exchanged, but more likely both patrols would scatter into the thick, tangled vegetation and redeploy in its cover. The Japanese riflemen would disperse to cover the flanks of their machine gunner. The Americans would bring forward automatic weapons to build up their firing line as they called for artillery or tried to outflank the Japanese. If the American artillery fire and movement were successful, the Japanese would flee, and the cavalrymen would move cautiously to finish off wounded Japanese. If the Japanese infantry proved too strong to expel, the Americans would withdraw, carrying their wounded and dragging their dead. As often as not, on first sight of each other, both sides would flee into the safety of the jungle.

Occasionally a single determined soldier could hold up ten or even one hundred men, as was the case during a drive against a nameless ridge. There a lone Japanese machine gunner blocked the advance of the center of the 112th's line. The cavalrymen had to deploy and work around the solitary gunner, thus precluding the use of friendly artillery to blast the hill. It was hard, slow, nerve-wracking combat, not at all glamorous, but exceedingly deadly, as fire was often exchanged at ranges of five meters or less. Robert Ross Smith described the nature of the fighting:

Each side complained that the other held isolated strong points, none of which appeared to be key positions. Both sides employed inaccurate maps, and both had a great deal of difficulty obtaining effective reconnaissance. In the jungle, broken terrain near Afua, operations frequently took a vague form, a sort of shadow boxing in which physical contact of the opposing sides was oft times accidental.

the 1st Mobile Fleet rendezvoused off the southern end of the Sulu archipelago on May 16, all the time watched and harassed by American submarines.

Preparations for the Capture of the Marianas

However, the Americans had plans of their own. They were already concentrating their forces at Eniwetok for Operation "Foragen," the conquest of the Marianas. The core of the assault force was Lieutenant General H. M. Smith's 127,000-man V Amphibious Corps of Vice Admiral Turner's 530-ship 5th Amphibious Force. The operation was opened by TF58, whose carrierborne aircraft swept over the Marianas and the adjacent waters on June 11 and 12. They destroyed 200 aircraft and sank at least 12 merchant ships before the battleships pounded shore installations.

The Marianas were the responsibility of Admiral Nagumo's Central Pacific Fleet, which had no ships and whose main subordinate formation was Lieutenant General Hideyoshi Obata's Japanese 31st Army.

The first target of "Forager" was Saipan, which was held by Lieutenant General Yoshitsugu Saito's force of 25,470 soldiers and 6,160 sailors. The assault was preceeded by a diversionary feint against Mutcho Point in the center of the island's west coast, whereas the real invasion beaches were farther to the south on each side of Charan Kanoa.

"Forager" Begins with the Landing on Saipan

Major General Thomas E. Watson's 2nd

An "Iowa" class battleship, either the *Iowa* or the *New Jersey*, lets rip with three 16-in shells during the naval bombardment of Saipan. Such bombardments played a key part in softening up Japanese targets before an invasion force landed. This naval fire was so accurate that it could be directed at specific stumbling blocks encountered by the advancing ground forces.

Marine Division landed on the left, and Major General Schmidt's 4th Marine Division on the right. The two divisions got ashore and established an initial beachhead without undue difficulty, but progress across the island was very slow because of stiffening Japanese resistance. On the third day of the battle, H. M. Smith decided to commit R. C. Smith's 27th Infantry Division, which landed to the right of the 4th Marine Division and drove east along the island's southern shore to reach Nafutan Point on June 28. Operating slightly farther north, the two marine divisions were later joined by part of the 27th Infantry as they advanced north to take the southern two-thirds of Saipan by June 30.

H. M. Smith was not happy with the performance of the 27th Infantry Division, which used more cautious army assault tactics than the two marine divisions. He replaced R. C. Smith first with Major General Sanderford Jarman and then with Major General George W. Griner. This caused considerable strife between the army and marine corps. Even so, the progress continued as the three divisions pushed the Japanese back into the northern end of the island. The 3,000 surviving Japanese made a final counterattack on July 7, and all organized resistance ended on July 9.

Allied losses were 2,521 killed, 8,912 wounded, and 798 missing, presumed dead. Japanese losses were horrendously higher: 2,000 captured and more than 27,000 dead. The dead list included Nagumo and Saito, who had committed suicide, and several hundred Japanese civilians who had leapt to death from cliffs rather than face capture.

The Battle of the Philippine Sea

One of the reasons for the fairly slow progress of the Saipan operation was the

Above: The first wave of marines hit the beach in Saipan on June 15, 1944. This was the first step in Operation "Forager," which was designed to provide territory where bases could be built for the Boeing B-29 Superfortress strategic bombers that were intended to tear the industrial heart out of Japan.

Left: Marine riflemen and a mortar crew shelter in foxholes and under the lee of a sandy bank during the Saipan fighting on June 25, 1944.

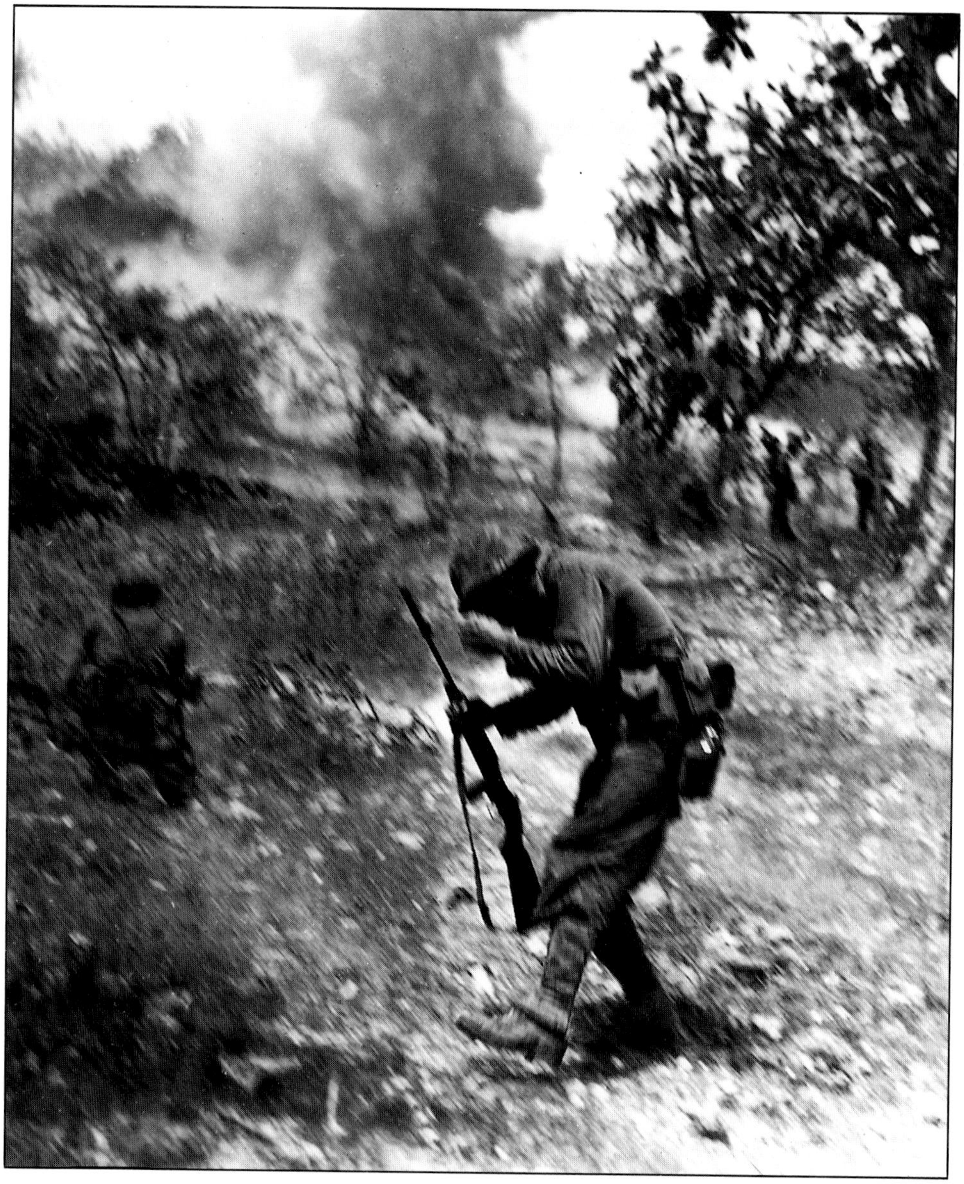

A marine staggers as he is hit by a piece of shrapnel from an exploding Japanese mortar bomb on July 2, 1944. By this time, the 2nd and 4th Marine Divisions had crossed Saipan from west to east, the 27th Infantry Division had come up on their right flank to clear the south of the island, and the Americans were now advancing to mop up resistance in the northern third of the island.

reduced scale of air support by TF58 from June 17. The aircraft carriers of TG58.2 and TG58.3, and then all other American warships, moved out for the Battle of the Philippine Sea, on their way rendezvousing with TG58.1 and TG58.4, which had earlier been detached for air strikes on Iwo Jima. These strikes had been delivered in June 16 to prevent Japanese aircraft staging through the island on their way to the Marianas, and the two Allied northern task groups now headed south to link up with the main strength of the 5th Fleet, which was under Mitscher's tactical command.

The Battle of the Philippine Sea was the result of Toyoda's strategic plan to destroy a major part of the Pacific Fleet. Japanese ships began to move from their bases at Tawi Tawi and Batjan toward the Philippine Sea as soon as word reached Toyoda of the landing on Saipan. Japan's 1st Mobile Fleet was made up of three fleet carriers, six light carriers, five battleships, ten heavy cruisers, two light cruisers, 22 destroyers, 24 submarines, and a fleet train of five tankers escorted by five destroyers. Boosted in strength by elements of the 5th Amphibious Force, the Allied 5th Fleet included seven fleet carriers, eight light carriers, seven battleships, eight heavy cruisers, 13 light cruisers, and 69 destroyers. In aircraft the Allies were wholly superior; not only were

Above: Hit by antiaircraft fire from the fleet carrier *Bunker Hill* and the light carrier *Cabot*, a Japanese plane plunges in flames during the Battle of the Philippine Sea on June 19, 1944.

Left: Harried by the attacks of American carrierborne attack aircraft, Japanese warships maneuver in tight turns during the Battle of the Philippine Sea. In the foreground, a heavy cruiser turns tightly in a counterclockwise direction.

The Japanese battleship *Kirishima*, the third of the four-strong "Kongo" class, was sunk on November 15, 1942. The class, designed in the United Kingdom by Sir George Thurston, embodied the lessons learned in the design of the British "Lion" class of battlecruisers. The lead ship was built in a British yard, and the other three were produced in Japanese yards. They were launched as pairs in 1912 and 1913. The ships were completed as battlecruisers, but after extensive reconstruction in 1930 and 1936, they were reclassified as battleships. The *Kirishima* displaced 31,980 tons, had an overall length of 729 ft 6 in, and her four seats of steam turbines delivered 136,000 hp to four propeller shafts for a maximum speed of 30·5 knots. The main battery had eight 14-in guns in four twin turrets, the secondary battery included fourteen 6-in guns in single turrets, and the antiaircraft battery totaled eight 5-in guns in four twin turrets and twenty 25-mm cannon in two twin mountings. The two units that survived Guadalcanal received steadily upgraded antiaircraft defense that eventually reached between ninety-four and one hundred and eighteen 25-mm cannon, even though the number of 5-in guns was reduced to 12.

Battle-weary marines move back from the front on Saipan during July 12, 1944, as fresh men march in the opposite direction to replace them.

Opposite: Naval support of landings on the Japanese-held Pacific islands always resulted in the exceptionally heavy use of ammunition. Just part of the 14-in shell supply for the ship's main battery is seen here on the deck of the battleship *New Mexico* before its transfer to the safety of the ship's magazines. The photograph was taken shortly before the ship participated in the operation to retake Guam during July 1944.

their planes considerably more advanced, but there were also 956 of them, to the 473 available to the Japanese. However, Ozawa planned the battle within range of land-based aircraft on Yap, Rota, and Guam, which would boost his air strength by about 100 aircraft.

The Mobile Force Vanguard (three light carriers and escorts) of the 1st Mobile Fleet was about 500 miles ahead of "A" and "B" Forces when its search aircraft detected the 5th Fleet at about daybreak on June 19. At about the same time, American fighters and antiaircraft guns were destroying waves of land-based Japanese attackers. Ozawa launched four waves of attack aircraft. When the first wave was detected, Mitscher launched his fighters to intercept. He then ordered his attack aircraft into the air to keep the Allied carrier decks clear of aircraft.

"The Great Marianas Turkey Shoot"

Shortly after this, an American submarine torpedoed the new fleet carrier *Taiho*, and just after noon another submarine torpedoed the *Shokaku*. Both carriers sank later in the day. The waves of Japanese attack aircraft were decimated by the fighters, and their remnants were almost completely destroyed by antiaircraft fire in what has become known as the "Great Marianas Turkey Shoot." Japanese losses were 346 aircraft, while the Americans lost just 30 machines.

As this fighting was raging over the 5th Fleet, Allied attack aircraft had reached and neutralized the Japanese airfields on Rota and Guam. Ozawa now broke away to the west, with Mitscher in pursuit. The Allies regained contact only in the afternoon of June 20, and Mitscher launched 216 aircraft which sank the light carrier *Hiyo* and two tankers, and also downed 65 Japanese aircraft for the loss of 20 of their own. With the aircraft almost out of fuel, the Allied pilots found it difficult to find and reach their carriers in the gathering darkness, despite the fact that Mitscher ordered their flight decks to be lit. About 80 aircraft ditched in the sea, but a destroyer sweep rescued about 50 of the downed aircrew.

Marines of the assault wave to push inland after the landing on Guam on July 21, 1944, duck as Japanese land mines explode and snipers open fire all around.

The Battle of the Philippine Sea finally destroyed any chance that Japan had to salvage anything from her increasingly precarious position. It also put a final end to the Japanese naval air arm, which lost more than 460 irreplaceable pilots.

The Capture of Guam...

The 5th Fleet returned to the Marianas to help in the operation on Saipan and to support the conquests of Guam and Tinian. Guam was held by a garrison of about 19,500 men under Lieutenant General Takeshi Takashina. The assault force was commanded by Major General Roy S. Geiger, and the campaign started with landings north and south of the Orote Peninsula on July 21. South of the peninsula, the landing force was Brigadier General Lemuel C. Sherpherd's 1st Provisional Marine Brigade, which was followed ashore by Major General Andrew D. Bruce's 77th Infantry Division. North of the peninsula, the landing was undertaken by Major General Turnage's 3rd Marine Division. These forces linked up behind the line of hills just inland from Guam's western side. They advanced north and eliminated the last pocket of organized Japanese resistance at Mount Machanao on the northwest tip of the island by August 10. The campaign cost the Americans 1,744 killed and 5,970 wounded, while the Japanese lost about 18,250 killed and 1,250 taken prisoner.

...Is Followed by the Fall of Tinian

After a diversionary feint against Sunharon Harbor on the island's southwest coast by Major General Watson's 2nd Marine Division, Tinian was actually invaded on its northwestern coast by Major General Clifton B. Cates's 4th Marine Division during July 24. The 9,000-man Japanese garrison, commanded by Colonel Keishi Ogata, fought with skill, determination, and a complete disregard for the inevitability of the Allied

Marines take cover amid fallen palm trees as they come under Japanese sniper fire on July 31, 1944. Once the snipers had been located, the area was blasted by naval gunfire and the advance was resumed.

success. The 4th Marine Division was supplemented by the 2nd Marine Division from July 25, and the last effective Japanese resistance was crushed in the southeast of the island on August 1. Allied losses were 394 killed and 1,961 wounded, while the whole Japanese garrison perished.

Strategic Differences Resolved

Meeting MacArthur and Nimitz at Pearl Harbor in July, President Roosevelt was faced with choosing between two plans designed to yield the same result, namely the surrender of Japan even if it meant invading the Japanese home islands. MacArthur proposed a descent on the Philippines for political reasons, as well as for the creation of a base from which to invade Japan. Nimitz proposed a descent on Formosa or even mainland China to create a comparable base area. In the end, Roosevelt opted for MacArthur's concept.

Army and navy planners then finalized the outline for two preliminary moves (MacArthur to Mindanao and Nimitz to Yap) before a joint descent on Leyte, and then a two-part exploitation (MacArthur to Luzon, and Nimitz to Iwo Jima and Okinawa). Nimitz allocated the Yap task to Halsey's 3rd Fleet, and Iwo Jima and Okinawa to Spruance's 5th Fleet. (It should be noted, however, that this apparent change in areas of responsibility was achieved not by movement of ships and fighting men, but by the exchange of commanders and their staffs so that what was the 5th Fleet now became the 3rd Fleet, TF58 became TF38, and the 5th Amphibious Force became the 3rd Amphibious Force.)

Morotai and Peleliu Fall to the Americans

As initial steps, MacArthur's forces occupied Morotai Island against little opposition on September 15, and Nimitz's

forces attacked objectives at the western end of the Palaus. Here Geiger's III Amphibious Corps landed on Peleliu on September 15, meeting furious resistance from a Japanese defense, commanded by Major General Sadal Inone, that was overcome only on October 13. On September 17, army troops of Vice Admiral Theodore S. Wilkinson's 3rd Amphibious Force landed on Angaur, which was secured by September 20. On September 23, Wilkinson occupied Ulithi Atoll, about 100 miles west of Yap, which provided a superb anchorage for the 3rd Fleet. Mopping up operations continued in the Palaus until November 25.

The Allied offensive between August 1944 and August 1945 completed the process of isolating Japan from its Southern Resources Area, and paved the way for the anticipated invasion of Japan.

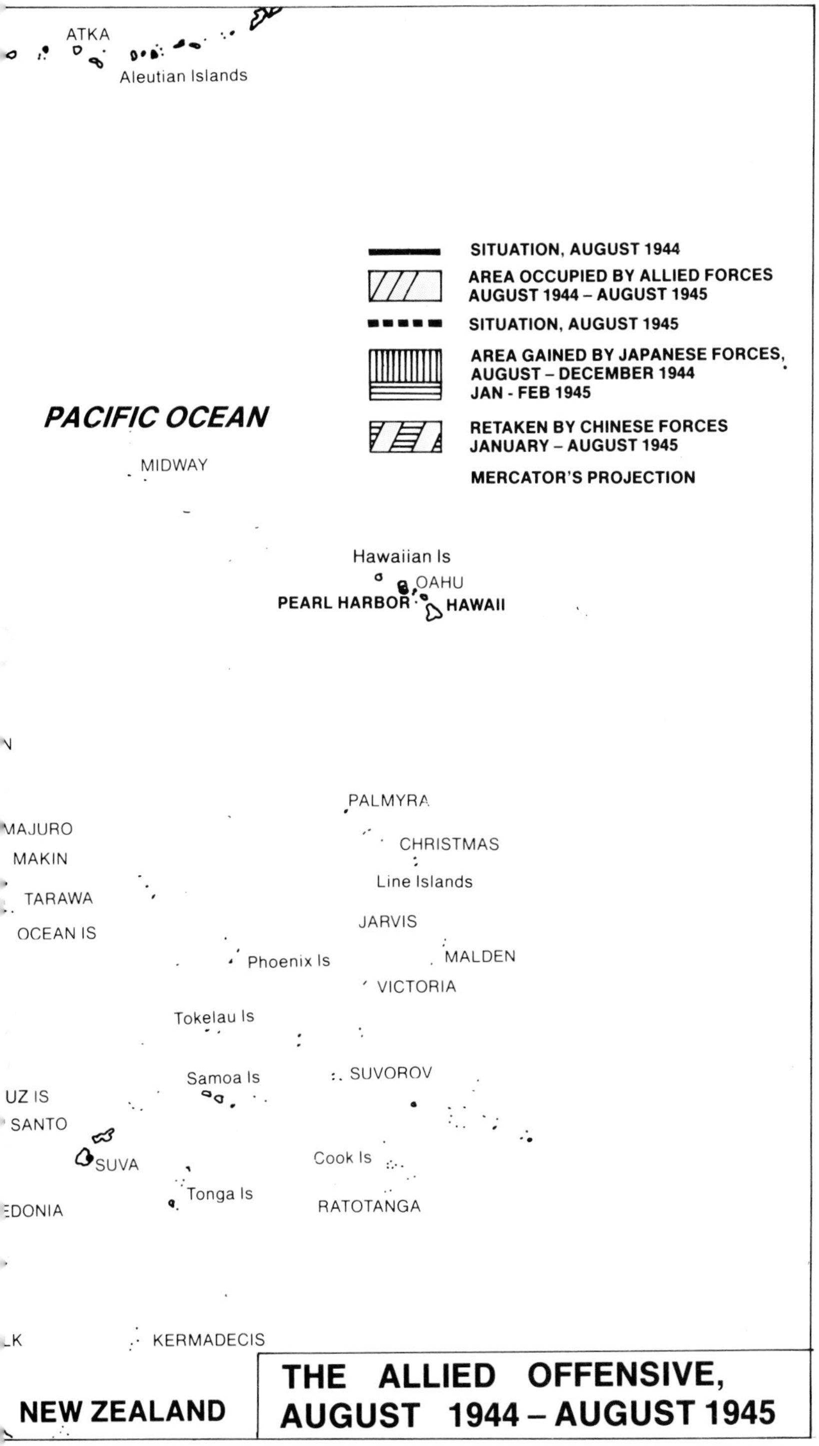

THE ALLIED OFFENSIVE, AUGUST 1944 – AUGUST 1945

Revised Plans

On September 15, the basic plan was modified in the light of information gathered during the course of 3rd Fleet operations. Sweeping through the Palaus from September 6, and then along the Philippine coast between September 9 and 13, the carriers had met little opposition. Halsey therefore suggested to Nimitz that the Mindanao and Yap landings were unnecessary. Nimitz agreed and suggested that MacArthur bring forward his invasion of Leyte. Nimitz offered to loan MacArthur his 3rd Amphibious Force and XXIV Corps, and MacArthur agreed to move up the Leyte operation from December 20 to October 20.

As MacArthur readied his forces, the 3rd Fleet swept north to paralyze the remnants of any Japanese air power that could be brought to bear. Moving out on October 7, Halsey struck at shipping and shore installations on Okinawa, and on October 11, he turned south toward Formosa and Luzon. The Japanese launched a major air effort from Formosa, and after hitting two cruisers and several other ships, they believed that they had crippled the 3rd Fleet. Detaching one carrier task group to escort the damaged ships to safety, Halsey took the rest of the 3rd Fleet into the Philippine Sea on October 15 in an effort to lure Japanese air strength into the area. Toyoda took the bait and sent 600 naval aircraft from Japan to Formosa. They were caught in a whirlwind of Allied air attacks that destroyed at least 300 aircraft in two days.

The offensive, which had been supplemented by 5th AAF attacks from New Guinea, 7th AAF raids from the Marianas, and XX Bomber Command sorties from China, claimed more than 650 Japanese aircraft for the loss of 75 American aircraft as well as damage to two cruisers and a few smaller ships.

Approach to the Philippines

The Philippines were held by the 350,000 men of General Masaharu Homma's Japanese 14th Area Army. The defense of the central and southern islands was entrusted to Lieutenant General Sosaku Suzuki's Japanese 35th Army, which had only the 16,000-man Japanese 16th Division on Leyte. The invasion force was made up of the 200,000 men of Krueger's 6th Army, carried and supported by the

Lieutenant, U.S. Naval Airforce, (Pacific) 1943-44

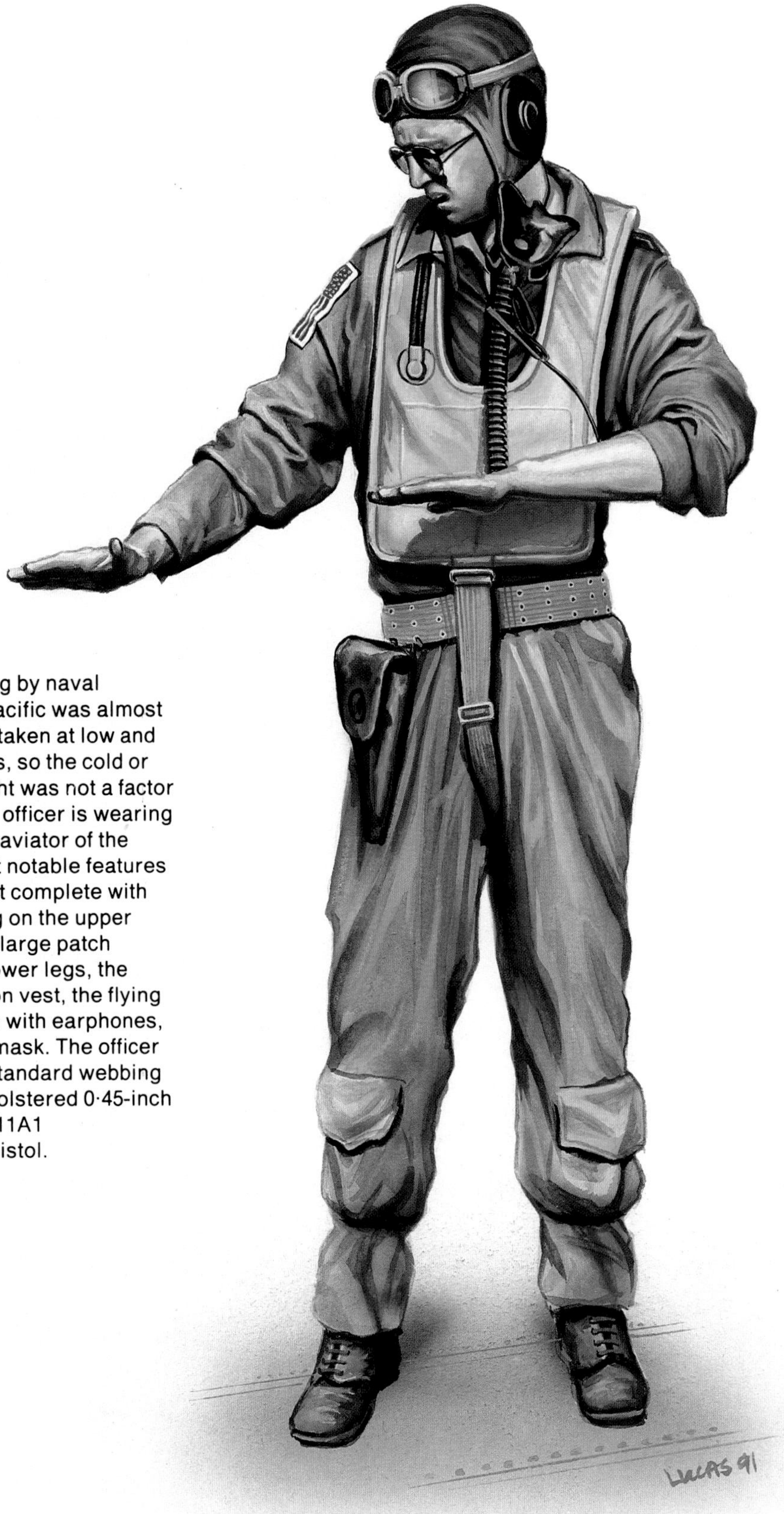

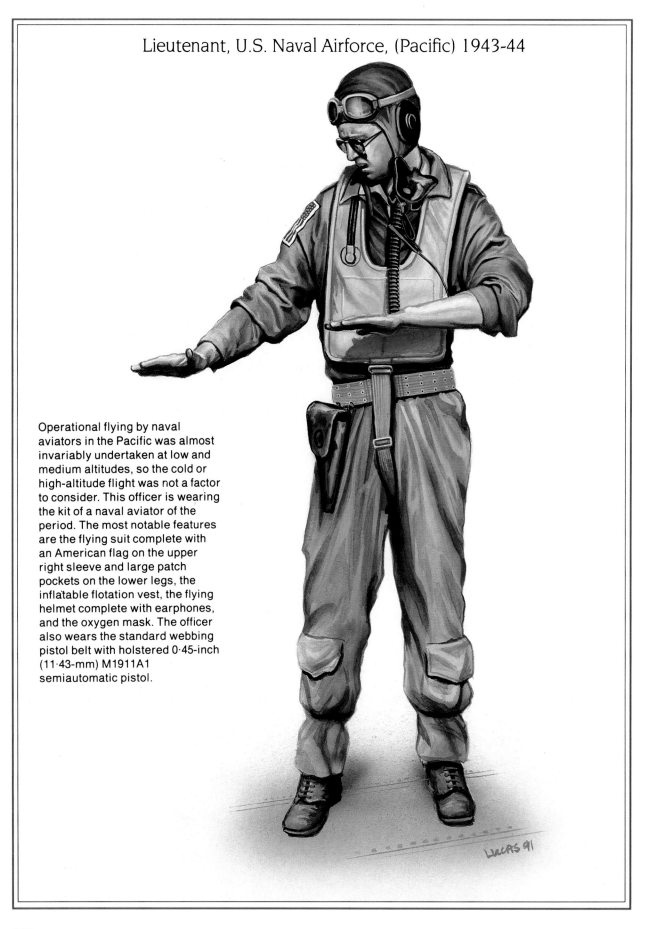

Operational flying by naval aviators in the Pacific was almost invariably undertaken at low and medium altitudes, so the cold or high-altitude flight was not a factor to consider. This officer is wearing the kit of a naval aviator of the period. The most notable features are the flying suit complete with an American flag on the upper right sleeve and large patch pockets on the lower legs, the inflatable flotation vest, the flying helmet complete with earphones, and the oxygen mask. The officer also wears the standard webbing pistol belt with holstered 0·45-inch (11·43-mm) M1911A1 semiautomatic pistol.

A U.S. soldier investigates the wreckage of a Mitsubishi A6M Zero fighter. At the beginning of the war, it was the world's finest carrierborne fighter, offering an exceptional blend of speed, range, and maneuverability. The Japanese planned for only a short war, so work on a successor was slow. As a result, the Zero flew on into an obsolescence in which large numbers were destroyed by increasingly skilled U.S. pilots flying far superior fighters.

700 vessels of Kinkaid's 7th Fleet, which included Wilkinson's 3rd Amphibious Force and Barbey's 7th Amphibious Force. Naval gunfire and air support were provided respectively by Rear Admiral Jesse B. Oldendorf's six elderly but reconditioned battleships, and Rear Admiral Thomas L. Sprague's 16 escort carriers, protected by nine destroyers and 11 destroyer escorts. Distant support was provided by Mitscher's TF38, which mustered eight fleet carriers, eight light carriers, six fast battleships, three heavy cruisers, nine light cruisers, and 58 destroyers. TF38's carriers had more than 1,000 aircraft.

The Landing on Leyte

The landing on the northeastern side of Leyte moved ahead without problem between October 20 and 22. Major General John R. Hodge's XXIV Corps on the left landed its 7th and 96th Infantry Divisions, and Major General Franklin C. Sibert's X Corps landed its 24th Infantry and 1st Cavalry Divisions on the right. Resistance was initially limited, and by October 30, the beachhead on Leyte and neighboring Samar had been expanded into a large lodgement filled with men and a mass of equipment and supplies.

By the time the initial landings had been completed, the Japanese had launched their final attempt to maintain the integrity of their military empire. Realizing that the American capture of the Philippines, Formosa, or the Ryukyus would sever the home islands from the Southern Resources Area, the Combined Fleet planned to use part of its scattered strength to decoy the Allied carrier force. This move would allow the rest of its strength to converge on the American landing area, destroy its amphibious capability, and strand its forces ashore.

As soon as American intentions became clear on October 17, the Japanese plan was put in motion. From Japan, Vice Admiral Ozawa's Mobile Force Strike Force steamed toward Luzon with one fleet carrier, three light carriers, two hybrid battleship carriers, three light

Right: The Japanese often turned areas honeycombed with caves into strong defensive complexes. In these circumstances, it proved less costly to the Americans to torch the cave entrances with flamethrower fire and then seal them with explosives. This photograph shows a flamethrower vehicle of the 1st Marine Division during the September 1944 fighting on Peleliu.

Below: An American carrier task group, with battleship and cruiser support, enters the fleet anchorage at Ulithi Atoll on December 12, 1944, after launching attacks on Japanese positions in the Philippines.

Iwo Jima
For further references see pages *111, 116, 117, 118,* 127

cruisers, and eight destroyers to decoy TF38's carriers away for the landing operation. The Japanese carriers were of no real fighting value, for they accommodated only 116 aircraft with very poorly trained crews.

The sacrifice of the Mobile Force Strike Force was designed to allow the rest of the Combined Fleet to fall on the 7th Fleet in a classic pincer movement. Sailing from the Ryukyus, Vice Admiral Shima's 2nd Strike Force of two heavy cruisers, one light cruiser, and seven destroyers was to link up with Vice Admiral Nishimura's "C" Force of Vice Admiral Kurita's 1st Strike Force from Brunei in northern Borneo. Supported by the ships of the 2nd Strike Force, "C" Force's two battleships, one heavy cruiser, and four destroyers were to pass south of Negros, Cebu, and Bohol islands before passing through the Surigao Strait to attack the 7th Fleet from the south. Kurita's own "A" and "B" Forces of the 1st Strike Force, also sailing from Brunei, were to pass through the Sibuyan Sea and San Bernardino Strait to attack the 7th Fleet from the north with two superbattleships, three battleships, ten heavy cruisers, two light cruisers, and 15 destroyers.

The Battle of Leyte Gulf

The result of these complex maneuvers was the Battle of Leyte Gulf, which took place between October 23 and 25. It was the world's largest ever naval battle, which unfolded in four related, but physically separate, engagements.

The Battle of the Sibuyan Sea

Moving up the western side of Palawan Island, Kurita's "A" and "B" Forces were detected by American submarines, which reported the situation to Halsey. They sank two heavy cruisers (the *Atago* and *Maya*) and severely damaged another (the

The scene aboard the light carrier *Belleau Wood* after she had been hit by a *kamikaze* plane on October 30, 1944. The hit caused severe damage, but the ship was repaired in time to participate in the Iwo Jima operation in February 1945.

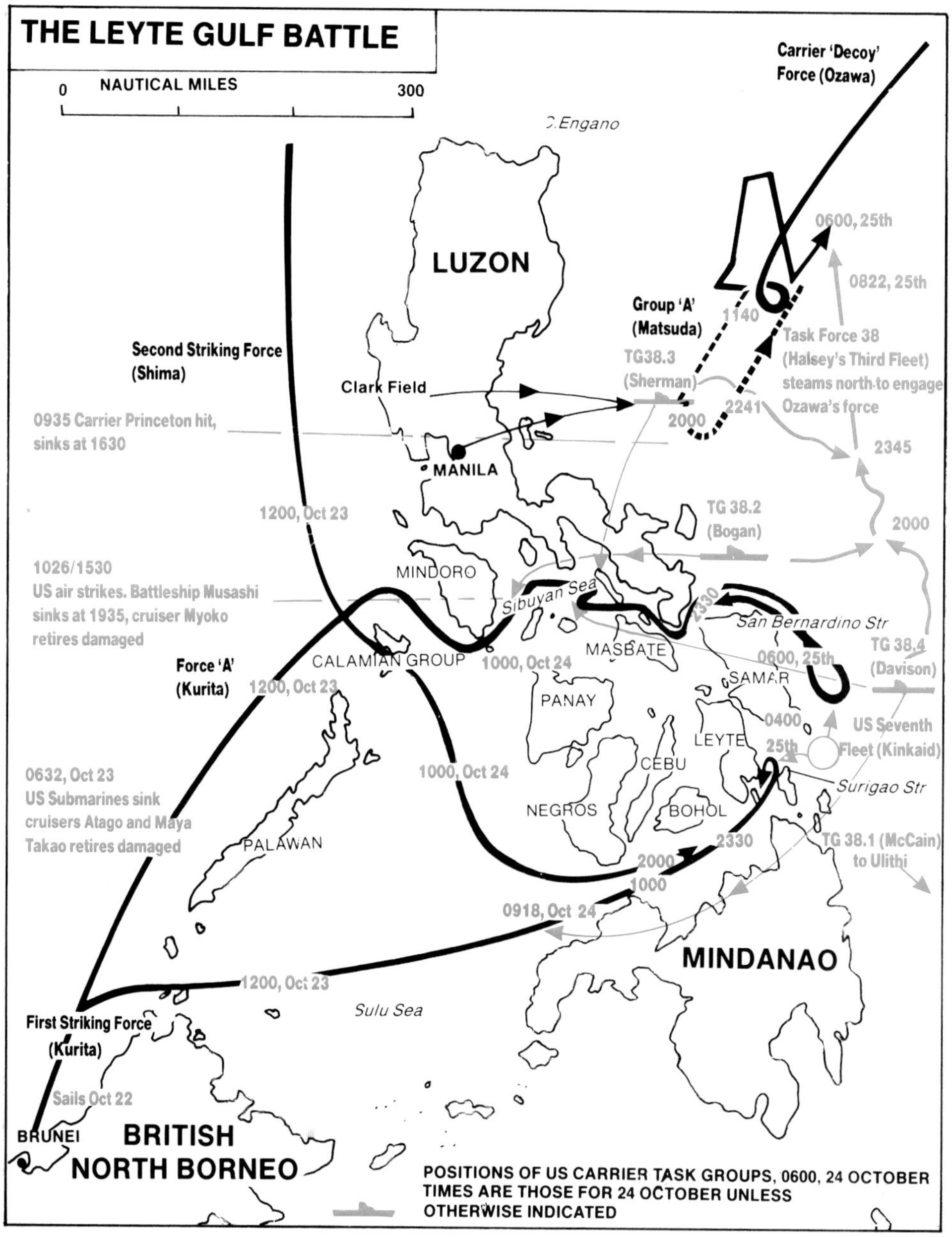

The four part battle of Leyte Gulf was the largest naval battle ever fought and resulted in a major U.S. victory.

Takao). As the Japanese ships moved into the Sibuyan Sea, aircraft from TG38.2, TG38.3, and TG38.4 attacked. In two days of incessant attack during the Battle of the Sibuyan Sea, the superbattleship *Musashi* was sunk and the heavy cruiser *Myoko* severely damaged before Kurita apparently reversed course to the west. After dark, however, the Japanese reversed again and made once more for the San Bernardino Strait. During October 24, attacks by Japanese land-based aircraft had sunk the light carrier U.S.S. *Princeton* and severely damaged the light cruiser U.S.S. *Birmingham*.

The Battle of Surigao Strait

The Battle of Surigao Strait took place on October 24 and 25. Warned of the approach of "C" Force and the 2nd Strike Force, Kinkaid placed Oldendorf's Battle Line in the strait with six battleships, three heavy cruisers, five light cruisers, and 29 destroyers, supported by 45 PT boats. Torpedo attacks by American destroyers sank the battleship *Fuso* and four destroyers before the rest of the Japanese ships ran into the concentrated gun and torpedo fire of Oldendorf's force

Seen from the escort carrier *Kitkun Bay*, Japanese shells bombard the doomed escort carrier *Gambier Bay*.

which sank the battleship *Yamashiro* and the rest of "C" Force with the exception of one destroyer. Bringing up the rear, the 2nd Strike Force ran into the massed fire of the PT boats, but pulled back in reasonable order, even though its light cruiser *Abukuma* was later torpedoed and sunk. Oldendorf did not pursue far, for he knew that the Battle Line might well be needed in Leyte Gulf.

The Battle off Samar

Kurita had meanwhile passed unopposed through the San Bernardino Strait, for Halsey's carriers had indeed been decoyed to the north by Ozawa's approaching carriers. Continuing around Samar, "A" and "B" Forces surprised Rear Admiral Clifton A. F. Sprague's TG77.4.3 (six escort carriers, three destroyers, and four destroyer escorts) in the Battle off Samar. Theoretically, Sprague's ships stood no chance against four battleships, six heavy cruisers, and some ten destroyers, but under cover of smoke and a rain squall, the Americans turned south at maximum speed in an attempt to outdistance the Japanese ships, which were considerably faster. Using lightly armed aircraft and destroyer attacks to harry and slow the Japanese, Sprague managed to escape with the loss of only one escort carrier, the U.S.S. *Gambier Bay*. The arrival of more aircraft from other American escort carrier task groups convinced Kurita that Halsey's carriers had returned to the area, and the Japanese withdrew, harassed by the aircraft of Rear Admiral John S. McCain's TG38.1, which had been detached to refuel at Ulithi, but was hastening back at top speed.

Later, the escort carrier U.S.S. *St. Lo* became the first ship sunk by land-based Japanese suicide aircraft, the dreaded *Kamikaze* that became so feared in later campaigns.

The Battle off Cape Engano

The last phase, the Battle off Cape Engano, took place on October 25. As TG38.2, TG38.3, and TG38.4 headed north, reconnaissance aircraft discovered Ozawa's Mobile Strike Force. Mitscher launched four waves of attack aircraft. Ozawa had sent nearly all his aircraft to operate from land bases and could oppose the American attackers only with antiaircraft guns. By nightfall, they had sunk the fleet carrier *Zuikaku* (last survivor of the Pearl Harbor Strike Force), the light carriers *Zuiho*, *Chitose*, and *Chiyoda*, and five other ships. Halsey had already sent back the six battleships, four cruisers, and eight destroyers of TF34 and the three fleet carriers and two light carriers, plus escorts, of TG38.2 to intercept Kurita. He finally turned

back with TG38.3 and TG38.4, allowing Ozawa's remaining strength of two battleships, two light cruisers, and six destroyers to escape.

The Battle of Leyte Gulf was a crushing defeat for the Japanese, who had deployed 64 ships and lost four carriers, three battleships, six heavy cruisers, four light cruisers, 11 destroyers, one submarine, and about 500 aircraft (carrier-borne and land-based), together with 10,500 men. The Allies had deployed 218 ships (including two Royal Australian Navy units) and their losses were one light carrier, two escort carriers, two destroyers, one destroyer escort, and about 200 aircraft, with 2,800 men killed and about 1,000 wounded.

Japanese resistance on Leyte began to stiffen on October 23, and between then and December 11, considerable reinforcements moved onto the island. Even so, the Allies continued to make progress, and all organized resistance ended on Christmas Day. By this time, the Allies had suffered 15,584 casualties,

Opposite Top: An American destroyer lays a smokescreen during the landings on Leyte.

Opposite Below: The key to the short-range defense of major U.S. warships against Japanese conventional air and *Kamikaze* attacks was the quadruple 40-mm Bofors mounting. This system could create a wall of explosive shells, and water cooling was used to keep barrel temperatures within specified limits.

while the Japanese had lost about 70,000 men.

Luzon Invaded

MacArthur's next objective was Luzon, which was invaded on January 9, 1945. The landing area was Lingayen Gulf. The 6th Army landed Major General Innis P. Swift's I Corps (6th and 43rd Infantry Divisions) on the left and Major General Griswold's XIV Corps (37th and 40th Infantry Divisions) on the right. Between January 10 and February 2, these divisions drove a deep pocket south toward Manila and then extended the American lodgement to the northeast.

Between January 30 and February 4, Lieutenant General Eichelberger's 8th Army started to make its presence felt. On January 30, elements of Major General Charles P. Hall's XI Corps landed at San Antonio and advanced to Olongapo and then Danulipihan, thereby cutting off the Bataan peninsula. On January 31, Major General Joseph M. Swing's 11th Airborne Division landed most of its strength on the beach at Nasugbu and pushed northeast toward Manila. Its progress was aided by an airdrop of the rest of the division on Tagaytay Ridge during February 3.

Manila was held by a force of 18,000 men under Rear Admiral Mitsuji Iwafuchi who ignored Yamashita's orders to pull out and decided to hold the city. Manila was isolated by February 4, but it was March 4 before the last defenders had been overcome. The battle left much of the city in ruins and resulted in the deaths of at least 16,665 Japanese.

Between February 16 and March 17, the Japanese garrisons on the islands in Manila Bay were eliminated. From March 15, the 6th Army waged a mountain

Right: Operating so far from its main bases in Hawaii and on the West Coast, the U.S. Navy made extensive use of special repair facilities such as this floating dock. This unit, located at an advance base, is here being used by the battleship *Pennsylvania*.

campaign against the rest of the 14th Area Army. Large areas were still in Japanese hands when Yamashita surrendered his last 50,000 men on August 15. Allied casualties in the Luzon campaign were 7,933 killed and 32,732 wounded, while the Japanese had suffered more than 192,000 killed and 9,700 captured in combat.

Clearing the Southern Islands

While the 6th Army was involved in the Luzon campaign, the 8th Army was concentrating on the recapture of the Visayas and the southern islands of the Philippine archipelago. This effort was complex and difficult, involving a mass of amphibious operations followed by fighting in very poor conditions and terrain. By the end of the war, the 8th Army had suffered 2,556 killed and 9,412 wounded. The Japanese had lost about 50,000 men killed, but they still held parts of Mindanao.

The POA's next move was to Iwo Jima, a small island needed as a forward air base for fighters escorting Marianas-based bombers on their way to or from Japan. Spruance replaced Halsey in overall command of what then became the 5th Fleet. Turner's 5th Amphibious Force was to carry and land Major General Schmidt's V Amphibious Corps, made up of the 3rd, 4th, and 5th Marine Divisions.

The Japanese had turned the barren island, covering only eight square miles, into a veritable fortress of concealed gun emplacements, concrete pillboxes, minefields, and barbed wire for the garrison of 22,000 army and navy soldiers commanded by Major General Tadamichi Kuribayashi.

Bloody Fighting for Iwo Jima

The Americans bombed Iwo Jima in a protracted campaign that achieved as little as the three-day naval gunfire barrage just before the landings on the southeast corner of the island. Schmidt

Men of the 4th Marine Division move inland from their beach area on the southeastern shore of Iwo Jima.

The beach of Iwo Jima is composed of black volcanic sand. The marines first met the strenuous Japanese defense of this small island here.

Above: A classic monument to one of the most celebrated events of the Pacific War, the raising of the American flag on Iwo Jima's Mount Suribachi.

Left: Men of the 5th Marine Division raise the American flag over the summit of Mount Suribachi on February 23, 1945.

used Major General K. E. Rockey's 5th Marine Division on the left and Major General Cates's 4th Marine Division on the right, with Major General G. B. Erskine's 3rd Marine Division in reserve to be landed later to take its place between the two assault divisions. On the first day, the marines suffered 2,420 casualties as they drove through to the western side of the island, separating the dominating feature of Mount Suribachi in the south from the rest of the Japanese garrison. Mount Suribachi was taken on February 23, and the marines then drove forward to the northern tip of the island, where the last Japanese defenders were overrun on March 25. The battle had been the bloodiest ever fought by the marines, who suffered casualties of 6,821 killed and 18,070 wounded. All of the Japanese were killed except for 1,083 taken prisoner.

The final step in Nimitz's progress was Okinawa, the largest of the Ryukyus.

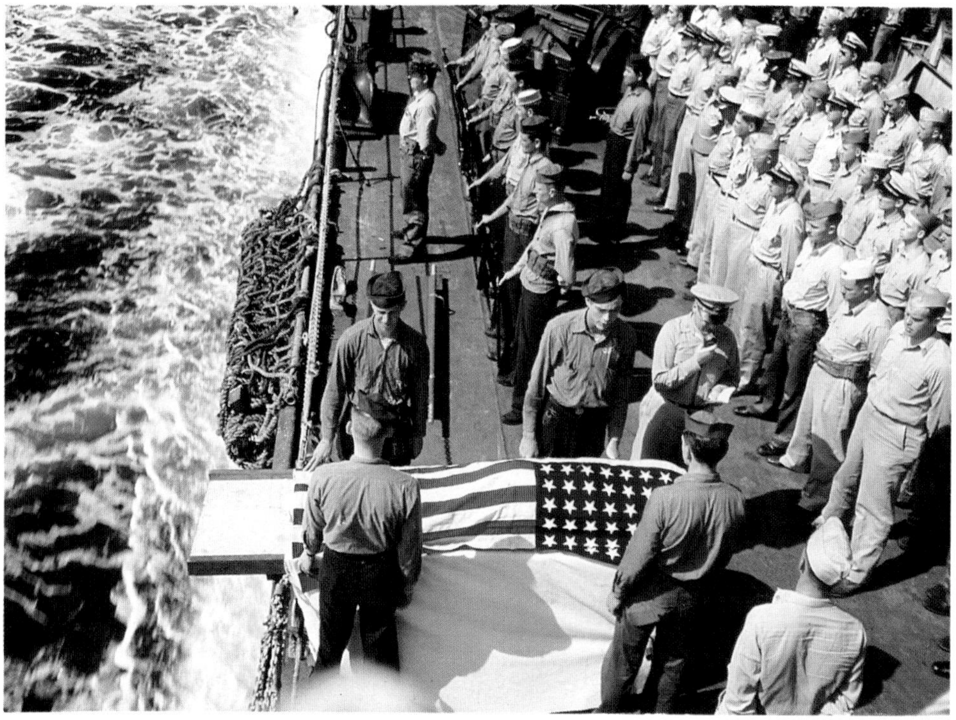

Some of the dead from the Iwo Jima fighting are buried at sea from the attack transport *Hansford.*

Opposite Top Left: Two Jima is a very small island whose conquest offered few tactical problems, but the operation still cost the U.S. forces heavy casualties.

A marine keeps his eyes open for Japanese snipers on Peleliu.

As part of Japan itself, the island was likely to be defended with tenacious bravery. Held by the 130,000 men of Lieutenant General Mitsuru Ushijima's Japanese 32nd Army, it contained a complex of formidable defensive positions amid a civil population of 450,000.

The American assault was Operation "Iceberg," which was scheduled for April 1. The 5th Fleet's 5th Amphibious Force carried and landed Lieutenant General Simon Bolivar Buckner's 10th Army. There were 180,000 men in the assault wave and reinforcements were available from New Caledonia. Between March 14 and 31, all Japanese air strength in the

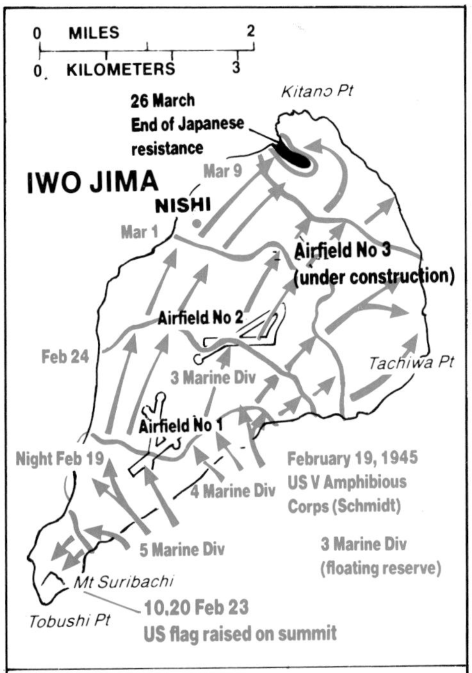

THE BATTLE OF IWO JIMA

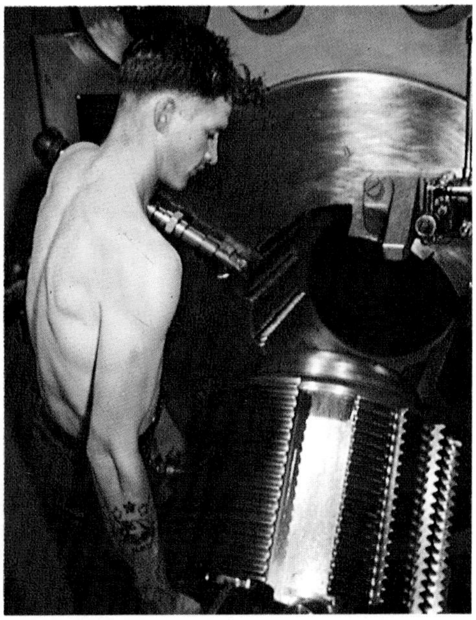

The gun captain opens the breech of one of the 16-in guns carried in the triple turret of a battleship. By the later stages of the war, U.S. battleships were still on the watch for Japanese ones, but they generally fired their main batteries at shore targets.

Below: The conquest of Okinawa was extremely bloody, but provided the U.S. forces with the springboard they might need for an invasion of Japan.

THE OKINAWA BATTLE

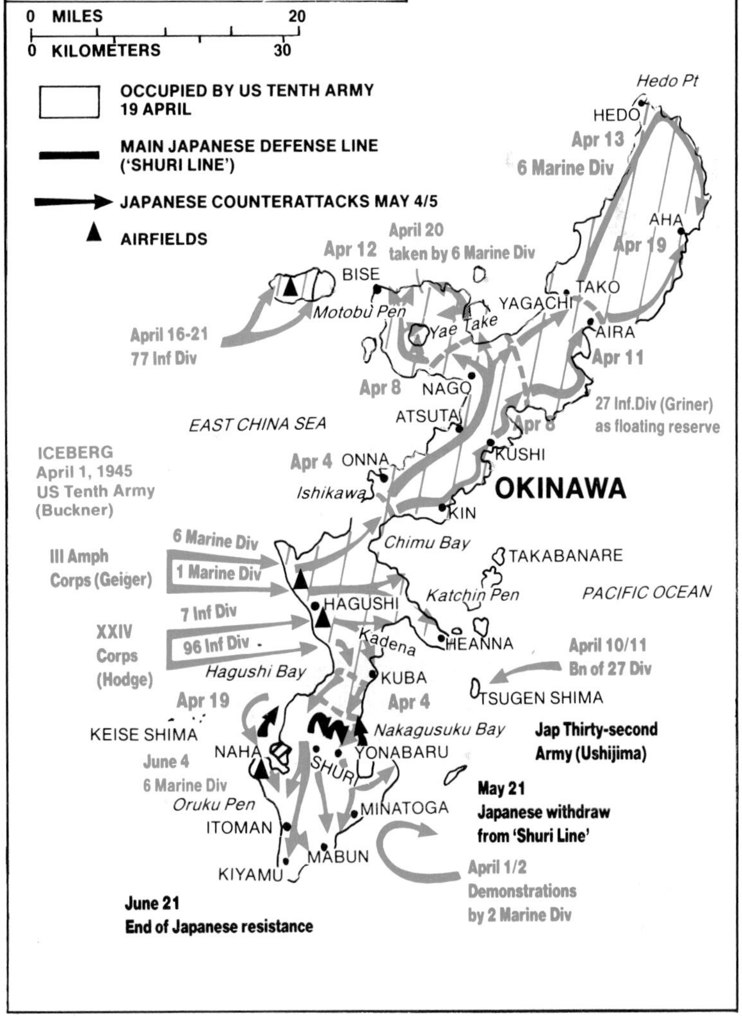

area was neutralized by American and British carrierborne aircraft, while land-based aircraft attacked Formosa and Japan. Between March 23 and 31, the defenses of Okinawa were bombarded by naval gunfire.

The Okinawa Campaign

On April 1, the 10th Army landed on the western side of the island, north and south of Hagushi, with Major General Geiger's III Amphibious Corps (6th and 1st Marine Divisions) on the left and Major General Hodge's XXIV Corps (7th and 96th Infantry Divisions) on the right. The marines drove straight across the island and then wheeled left to overrun the northern part by April 13. Neighboring Ie Shima Islet was taken by the 77th Infantry Division between April 16 and 21. The two army divisions had an altogether rougher time as they wheeled right and came up against the Machinato Line of the defensive zone around Shuri. The two divisions finally broke though this line, only to encounter the defenses of the Shuri Line, and further furious fighting followed before the Japanese fell back on May 21. On June 4, the Japanese left flank

was turned by the amphibious delivery of the 6th Marine Division onto the Oruku Peninsula south of Naha, the main city of Okinawa. Effective resistance ended on June 21. Okinawa was in American hands as a springboard for the planned invasion of Japan, but the campaign had been costly. The Japanese had suffered casualties of 107,500 known dead plus another 20,000 or so sealed into deep caves during the fighting, and 7,400 men taken prisoner. The 10th Army lost 7,374 men killed and 30,056 wounded.

At the same time, the navy had lost 5,000 men killed and 4,600 wounded as a result of the Japanese navy's last naval air offensive, which had also cost the 5th Fleet 36 vessels sunk and 368 damaged,

Right: After using ordinary warplanes loaded with explosives as *kamikaze* platforms, the Japanese developed a special weapon for the role, the Yokosuka MXY-7. The type was called *Okha* (Cherry Blossom) by the Japanese, but the Americans rapidly adopted the name *Baka* (Fool). It was designed to be launched from beneath a "mother" plane and then dive onto its target under rocket power. This example was captured on Okinawa.

Opposite Top: During the fighting on Okinawa a marine fires his flamethrower at a Japanese soldier who refused to abandon the tomb he was using as a sniper's nest.

Opposite Below: A *kamikaze* plane is seen just feet from the side of the battleship *Missouri* off Okinawa.

Overleaf: The battleship *Iowa* refueling at sea from the tanker *Cahaba*. Launched in May 1943 and displacing 5,730 tons, she was one of the many ships that formed the fleet train for the U.S. warships in the Pacific Ocean. Such tankers, ammunition ships, store ships, water distillation ships, and hospital ships played a decisive part in allowing the Pacific Fleet to undertake sustained operations many thousands of miles from the nearest major base.

as well as 763 aircraft destroyed. Multitudes of *kamikaze* aircraft were used, as well as the one-way trip of the superbattleship *Yamato*, which was meant to strand herself amid the invasion fleet and pound away with her guns until she was destroyed. However, the ship was detected and sunk by Allied aircraft on April 7 before she reached Okinawa.

Allied planners now settled down to the task of designing the invasion of Japan, which was conceived in two parts. Operation "Olympic," scheduled for November 1, 1945, envisaged the invasion of the southern island of Kyushu by the 6th Army with four corps controlling 13 divisions. Operation "Coronet," scheduled for March 1, 1946, was less firm, but foresaw the invasion of the main island of Honshu by the 1st Army (three corps with eight divisions) and the 8th Army (two corps with six

Right: One of the most important weapons against Japanese air power was the "parafrag," or parachute-retarded fragmentation bomb. It could be dropped accurately at low level. The parachute slowed its descent, which allowed the bomber to escape before the bomb hit the ground and detonated, showering the area around it with high-velocity fragments.

Opposite Bottom: Seen here fitting out at Kure naval base in September 1941, the *Yamato* was a superb battleship, but was finally used (and wasted) in an attempted sea *kamikaze* mission against the U.S. invasion forces off Okinawa.

divisions). The fighting was expected to be bloody in the extreme, and 1,500,000 casualties were projected. As these plans were prepared, Japan was pounded by American aircraft in a strategic bombing campaign that finally made the invasion of Japan unnecessary.

Strategic Bombing of Japan

The first strategic raid against Japan had been mounted on June 15, 1944, when B-29s took off from the five airfields of the huge base complex built by local labor at Chengtu in China and struck at steel production in Kyushu. The B-29s had moved to India between April and May 1944 as the first element of the new XX Bomber Command and had been blooded in raids against targets in Southeast Asia. Under the command of Major General Curtis E. LeMay, XX BC became an increasingly powerful and effective force between June and December 1944. Fuel and weapons had to be airlifted to the Chengtu base from India, but targets were struck in areas as widespread as Formosa, Kyushu, and Manchuria.

As soon as possible after the capture of the Marianas, Boeing B-17

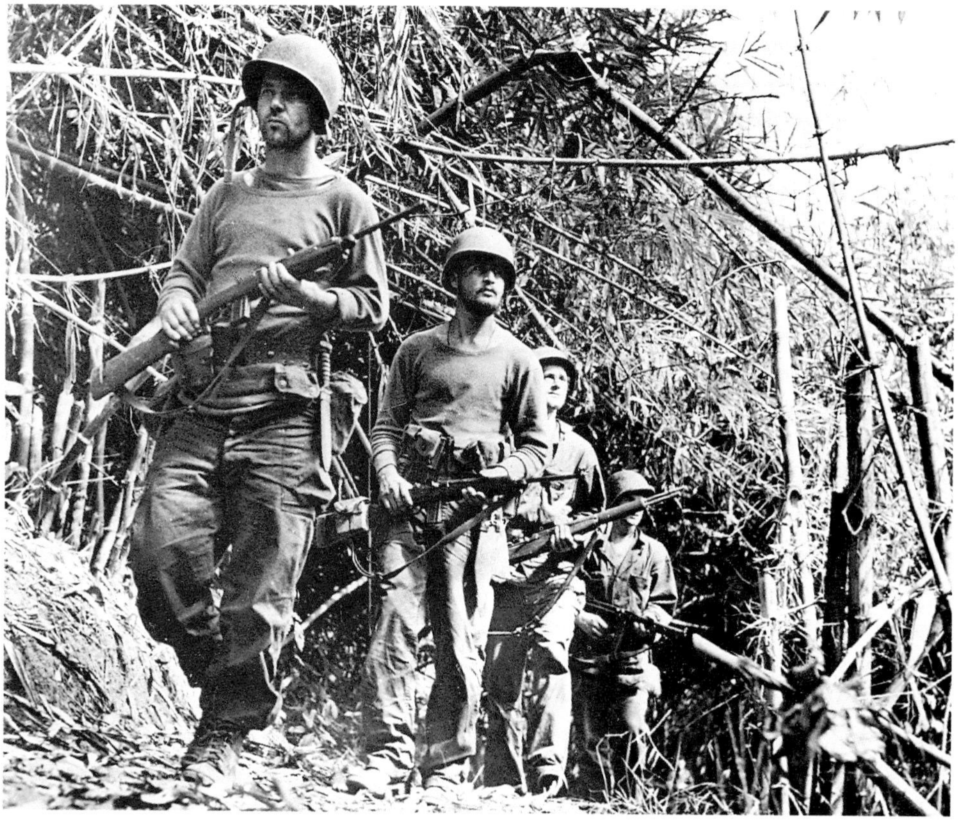

Right: One of the areas where only a small number of Americans fought was Burma, which was primarily a British theater. In the north of the country, however, the Chinese contributed several divisions supported by the 5307th Provisional Infantry Regiment. Otherwise known as "Merrill's Marauders" after its first commander, Brigadier General Frank D. Merrill.

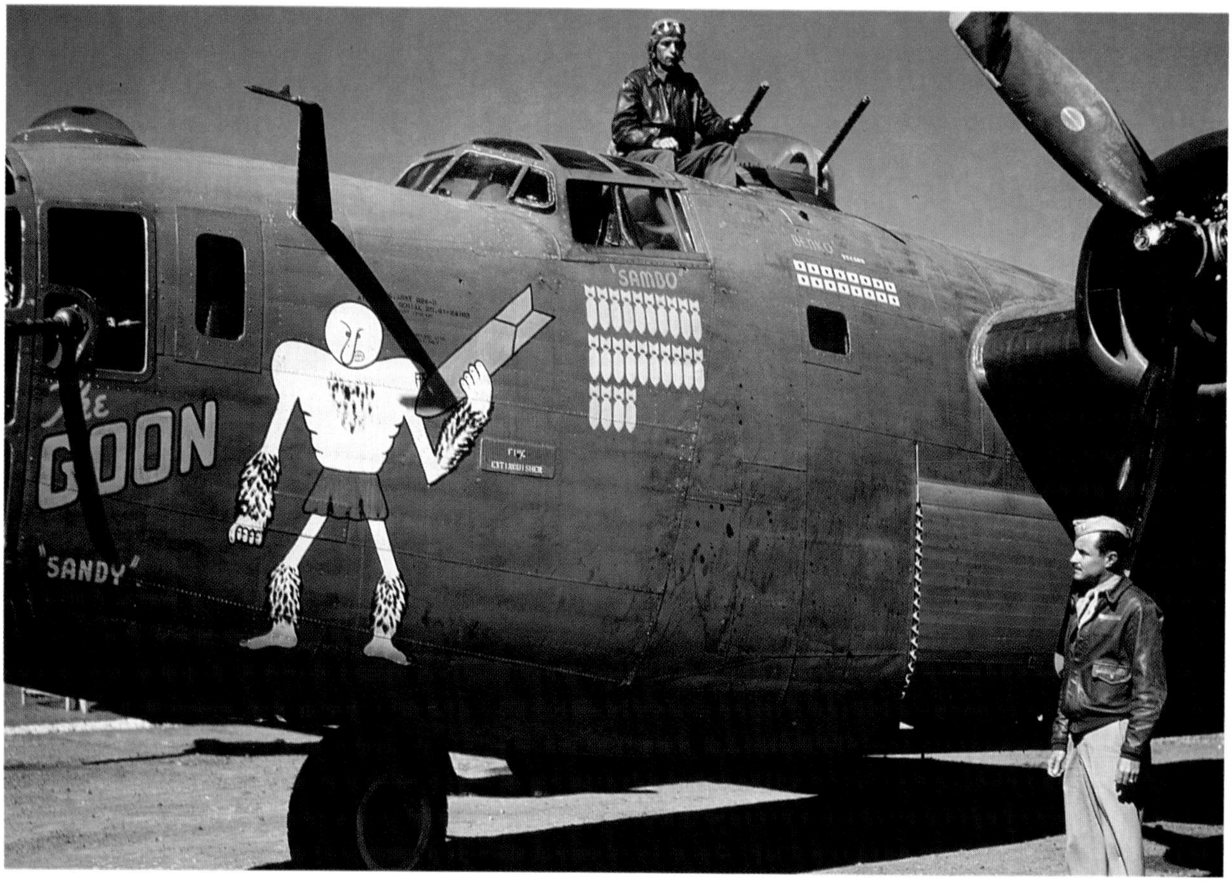

Below: The China Air Task Force, and later the 14th Army Air Force, achieved useful results with bombers such as this Consolidated B-24 Liberator named *The Goon*.

Right: Japanese troops surrender to a U.S. Marine under a white flag of truce.

Below: It was only after the end of the war and their occupation of Japan that the Americans saw at close hand the devastating results of their strategic bombing campaign. This is the wreckage of a drydock at the major naval base and construction yard at Kure. Some of the 59 two-man midget attack submarines can be seen in the dock, which was flooded by the Americans soon after their arrival in Kure.

Operating from bases in the Marianas, U.S. heavy bombers ripped the industrial and urban heart out of Japan in the period between February and August 1945.

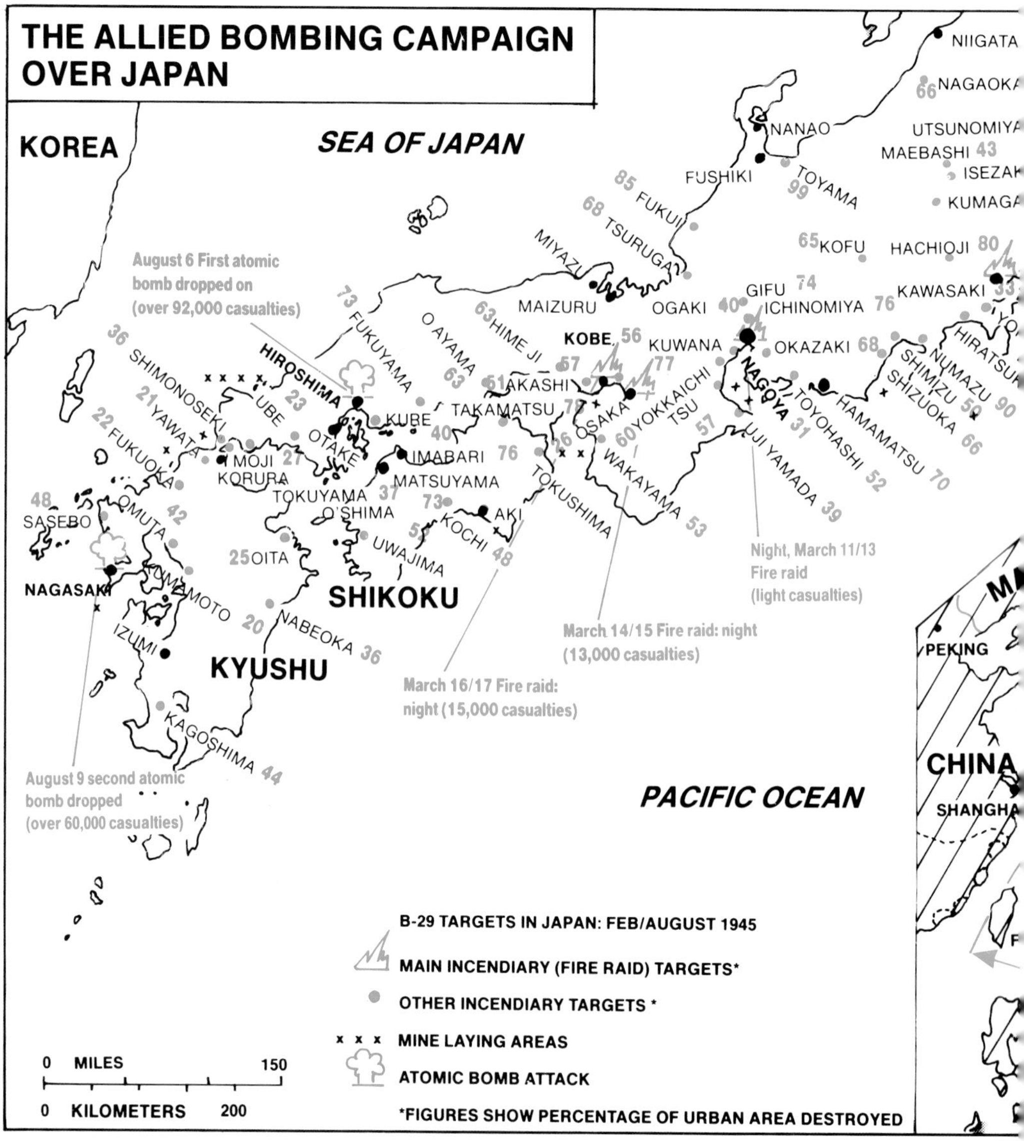

Flying Fortresses and Consolidated B-24 Liberators moved into captured Japanese airfields for a campaign against the Japanese in the Bonins and Iwo Jima. Meanwhile engineers constructed huge new airfields on the islands for the B-29. During October 1944, the new XXI BC moved into the Marianas, flying its first mission on October 28 with what were in effect training sorties against Truk.

XXI BC flew its first mission against Japan on November 24, when more than 100 aircraft struck at an aircraft plant near Tokyo. For the rest of the month and the whole of December, XXI BC struck with between 100 and 120 bombers every five days or so, dropping high explosive bombs from high altitude, normally about 30,000 feet. This was not an effective tactic; high winds in the region severely affected bombing accuracy. Japanese fighters also managed to shoot down about six percent of the bombers, an unacceptably high figure.

In January and February 1945, the nature of the bombing campaign was reassessed. The campaign was having some effect. It was destroying some of Japan's war-making industries and reducing the output of workers, who were frequently disturbed by alarms, if not by actual raids. But losses were too high, and bombing was not accurate enough. It was decided to gather both

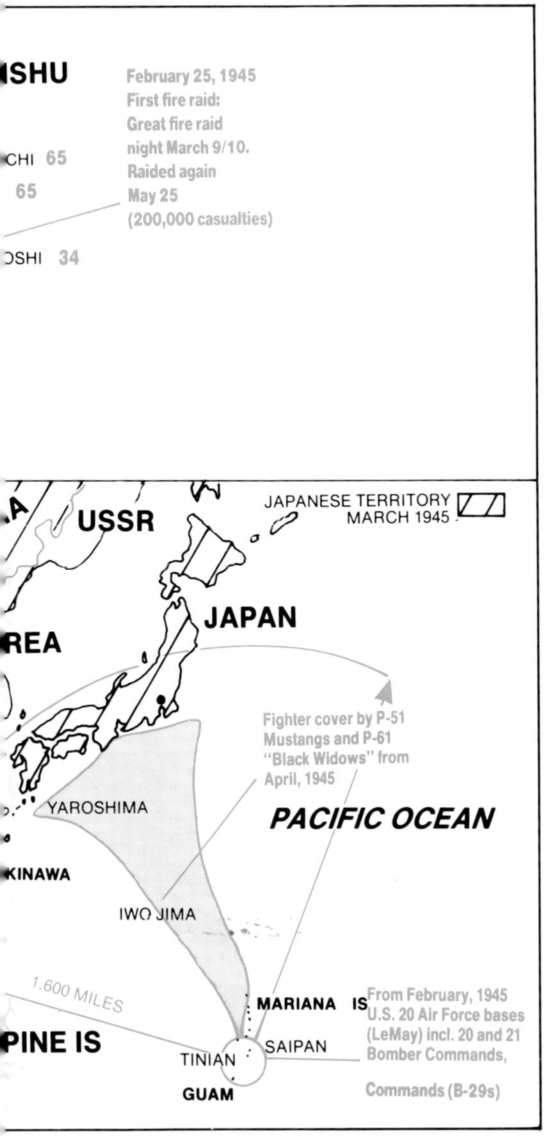

XX and XXI BCs, the two subordinate formations of Major General Nathan F Twining's 20th AAF, in the Marianas.

Revised tactics

To improve the efficiency of XXI BC while XX BC was moving to the Marianas, LeMay took over as commander. In February and March, LeMay introduced a new bombing tactic. Low-altitude night raids with incendiary bombs replaced high-altitude day attacks with high explosive bombs. The new system was fully vindicated on March 9/10, when 334 B-29s attacked Tokyo. Flying at about 7,000 feet, the bombers unloaded 1,667 tons of incendiaries in what unfolded as the single most destructive air raid of history. Much of Tokyo was built of wood, and the incendiaries started a firestorm that gutted the Japanese capital, in the process killing 83,000 people and injuring another 100,000 or more. This pattern of raid was repeated another four times in the following ten days.

At low level, the bombers could carry three times the payload they could lift to high altitude, and the low-level night attacks were far less prone to interception than the earlier high-altitude day attacks. Losses dropped, while bombing effect increased dramatically. The five raids of the period between March 9 and 19 delivered 9,365 tons of bombs. Thirty-two square miles of Tokyo were destroyed, with a loss of only 22 aircraft, a mere 1·4 percent of the 1,595 sorties.

From April 7, the bombers could be escorted by North American P-51 Mustang fighters of VII Fighter Command, now based on Iwo Jima. As a result, the B-29s could also undertake daylight raids at

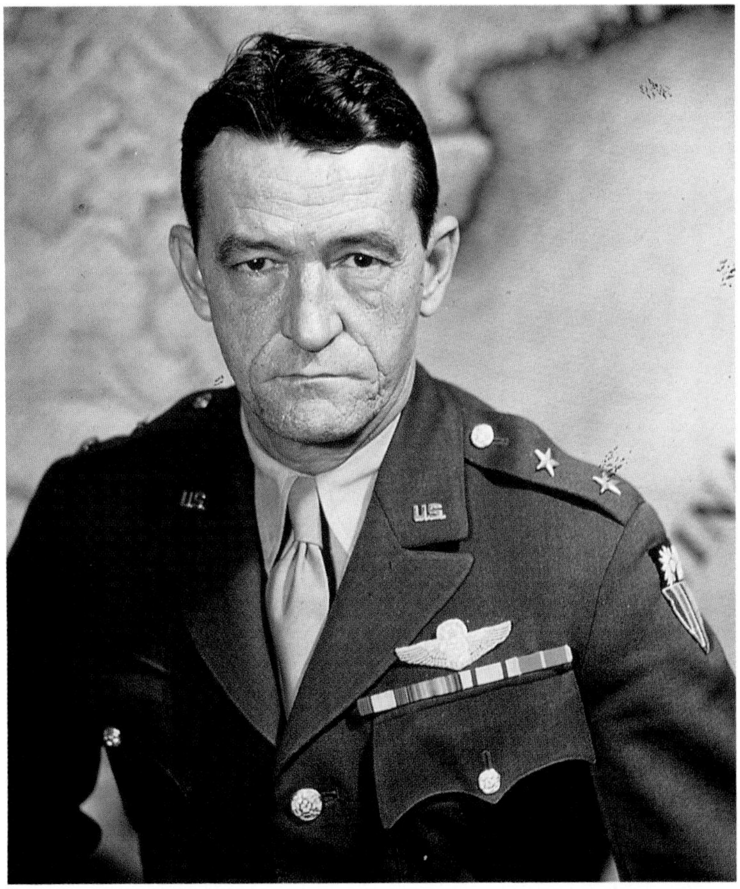

The officer who commanded American airmen for the longest time in China was Claire L. Chennault, seen here in the rank of major general.

The mushroom cloud rises over the devastation caused by the atomic bomb dropped on Nagasaki on August 9, 1945. Stunned by the atomic blast that had destroyed Hiroshima three days earlier, the Japanese were galvanized by this second catastrophe to press for a ceasefire while surrender negotiations were opened.

The ruins of Nagasaki photographed on May 22, 1946.

The devastation of Hiroshima. Japan's urban and industrial centers were effectively wiped out by conventional bombing, and the seal was set on this process by the atomic bombings of Hiroshima and Nagasaki.

Photographed in September 1945, Nagasaki had been virtually wiped out by the second atomic bomb. In the foreground is a radiologist at Nagasaki Hospital, Dr. Nagai, who died a few days later as a result of radiation sickness.

Late in the war, American carrier groups were able to operate close to the Japanese home islands and add the weight of their air groups' bombs to the loads delivered by Boeing B-29 Superfortresses. This Curtiss SB2C Helldiver dive-bomber is seen over the ruins of Tokyo on August 28, 1945, just days after the end of hostilities.

Japanese prisoners-of-war on Guam bow their heads as they hear of Emperor Hirohito's announcement of Japan's unconditional surrender on August 15, 1945.

medium altitude. These raids proved effective in themselves, and they also tempted Japan's obsolescent fighters into the air, where they could be destroyed by the P-51s.

Between May and August, the strategic campaign climaxed after XX BC had been installed on the Marianas in April. Japan's five largest and industrially most important cities (Tokyo, Nagoya, Kobe, Osaka, and Yokohama) were completely destroyed, and the problems of crushed industries and severed communications were made worse by the millions of homeless. Japan was on the verge of complete disaster, but refused even to consider surrender.

On July 16, 1945, the Americans exploded the world's first atomic device at Alamogordo in the New Mexico desert. It

was clearly the decisive weapon that had been anticipated by those involved in this top secret project, and the 509th Composite Group was created to deliver the new weapon.

Top Left: The funeral procession of President Franklin D. Roosevelt passes along Washington's Constitution Avenue on April 14, 1945.

Atom Bombings End World War II

President Roosevelt died on April 12, 1945, and Vice President Harry S Truman succeeded to the presidency. It was Truman who made the decision to use "the bomb." On August 6, a single weapon was dropped on Hiroshima, wiping out the center of the city and causing casualties of 78,150 dead and 70,000 injured. As the stunned Japanese tried to come to grips with the catastrophe, another bomb was dropped on Nagasaki during August 9, killing 40,000 people and injuring 25,000 more.

On August 10, Japan offered to surrender, and hostilities ceased on August 15. On September 2, Japanese officials signed the official surrender on board the battleship U.S.S. *Missouri* in Tokyo Bay, and World War II was over.

Below: Nomoru Shigemitsu, the Japanese foreign minister, signs the instrument of Japan's surrender on board the battleship *Missouri* in Tokyo Bay on September 2, 1945. The ceremony is witnessed by other members of the Japanese delegation and by a large number of Allied officers including General of the Army Dougla MacArthur, who broadcasts details of the event.

Glossary

Aircraft carrier: The type of warship that took over from the battleship as the world's most important large ship during World War II. In essence it is a floating airfield which provides hangars and maintenance facilities for a substantial number of aircraft. In World War II, the aircraft carrier was developed in three main forms: the fleet carrier, displacing between 20,000 and 45,000 tons for operations with up to 100 aircraft; the light carrier, displacing between 12,500 and 20,000 tons for operations with up to 50 aircraft; and the escort carrier, displacing less than 12,500 tons and used for antisubmarine, escort, or amphibious support operations with up to 25 aircraft.

Army group: Largest field formation, made up of two or more armies.

Battalion: A basic subdivision of the regiment, generally less than 1,000 men and commanded by a lieutenant colonel.

Battle-cruiser: A capital ship combining characteristics of both battleship and cruiser. It is armed as a battleship but has the performance of a cruiser because the battleship's effective but very heavy armor protection has been eliminated.

Battleship: A major ship of World War II, with heavy armament and heavy protection.

Beachhead: The designated area on an enemy shore which is seized and held in an amphibious assault to guarantee that additional troops, equipment, and supplies can be landed to create a lodgement.

Blockade: A naval campaign to deny the enemy or neutrals access to or departure from the enemy's ports and coast.

Brigade: A basic subdivision of the division, made up of two or more regiments and commanded by a brigadier general.

Corps: A primary unit of the army, including two or more divisions and commanded in the U.S. Army by a major general (but in most other armies by a lieutenant general).

Cruiser: A long-range warship intermediate in size and displacement between the destroyer and the battleship. It developed in two primary forms: the light cruiser with 6-inch guns for commerce raiding, and the heavy cruiser with guns of 8-inch or greater caliber for fleet operations.

Destroyer: A comparatively small warship developed from the torpedo boat with a main armament of torpedoes and guns of about 5-inch caliber. Used for independent or fleet operations, the destroyer relies on speed and agility to avoid enemy fire instead of armor to withstand such fire.

Dive-bomber: An airplane designed to dive almost vertically toward its target, dropping a single large bomb with extreme accuracy before pulling up into a climb away from the target.

Division: The smallest army formation, including two or more regiments (brigades in British divisions) and commanded by a major general. As the basic organization designed for independent operation, it contains support elements (artillery, engineers, etc.) in addition to its infantry.

Fighter: An airplane designed to fight other aircraft. It is comparatively small and nimble, with a battery of machine guns set to fire directly ahead along the pilot's line of sight.

Flank: The extreme right or left side of a body of troops in a military position.

Flying boat: An airplane designed for waterborne operation. It has a boat hull so that it floats directly in the water without intervening floats. Flying boats were sometimes produced in amphibious form with retractable wheeled landing gear to improve their operational versatility.

Formation: Any large body of troops capable of operations independent of the rest of the army. In addition to its organic infantry units, it has a full range of artillery, engineer, and support services. The smallest formation is generally the division.

Lodgement: The name given to a beachhead after it has been consolidated and expanded to incorporate airfield, port, and communications facilities. Major formations strong enough to sustain offensive operations against the enemy can be created from the lodgement.

Logistics: The science of planning and carrying out the movement of forces and their supplies.

Materiel: The overall term for equipment, stores, supplies, and spares.

PT boat: A small craft designed to carry out torpedo attacks on larger warships. It has speed and agility, and a main armament of two or four torpedoes carried in fixed deck launchers.

Regiment: A basic tactical unit subordinate. A regiment is part of a division (in British service the brigade) and includes two or more battalions generally commanded by a colonel.

Seaplane tender: A vessel designed to operate floatplane aircraft, either launched with the aid of a catapult, or lowered to the water by crane for conventional take-off; after landing on the water, seaplanes were recovered by crane.

Strategy: The art of planning major operations in a campaign or war.

Submarine: A warship that can submerge and operate under the surface for a long period. In World War II, such boats had diesel-electric propulsion that limited underwater endurance to about 24 hours. Its main armament was the long-range torpedo, a decisive weapon in the American campaign against Japan's merchant marine and navy.

Tactics: The art of planning minor operations in a battle.

Torpedo bomber: An airplane designed to launch a low-level torpedo against enemy ships. In World War II, such aircraft were also used as level bombers with conventional free-fall bombs.

Unit: A small body of troops organized without the capability to operate independently from the rest of the army. Therefore it does not have in addition to its organic infantry units a full range of artillery, engineer, and support services. The largest unit is the brigade.

Bibliography

Benedict, Ruth. *The Chrysanthemum and the Sword: Patterns of Japanese Culture.*
(Houghton Mifflin, Boston, 1989).
Outstanding social history describing the Japanese warrior mentality. Essential for understanding America's Pacific enemy.

Bradley, John H. and Dice, Jack W. *The Second World War: Asia and the Pacific.*
(Avery Publishing Group, Wayne, NJ, 1989).
A concise one-volume text coordinated with a good map book.

Falk, Stanley L. *Bataan: The March of Death.*
(New York, 1962).
A balanced account of this dreadful event.

Falk, Stanley L. *Decision at Leyte.*
(W. W. Norton & Co., New York, 1966).
Air, sea, and land battles that finished Japan.

Hammel, Eric. *Guadalcanal: The Carrier Battles.*
(Crown Publishers, New York, 1987).
The all important air-sea battles that determined the island's fate.

Hersey, John. *Hiroshima.*
(Alfred A. Knopf, New York, 1985). The classic account about the dropping of the world's first A-bomb.

Lawson, Ted W. *Thirty Seconds Over Tokyo.*
(Random House, New York, 1953).
Popular history about the Doolittle raid.

Lord, Walter. *Day of Infamy.*
(New York, 1965).
A good popular history of Pearl Harbor.

Mason, John T., Jr. *The Pacific War Remembered.*
(Naval Institute Press, Annapolis, MD, 1986).
Oral histories.

Morison, Samuel Eliot. *The Struggle for Guadalcanal, August 1942-February 1943.*
(Boston, 1950).
Excellent naval history of the great American counter-offensive; however, written before the disclosure of the role of Magic.

Pyle, Ernie. *Ernie's War, The Best of Ernie Pyle's World War II Dispatches.*
(Random House, New York, 1986).
America's best regarded combat reporter who died with the soldiers he loved on a Pacific island.

Scott, Robert L. *God is My Co-Pilot.*
(Charles Scribner's Sons, New York, 1943).
A classic story of a fighter pilot with the Flying Tigers.

Stafford, Edward P. *The Big E.*
(Random House, New York, 1962).
The story of the only U.S. carrier to serve the entire Pacific war.

Steinberg, Rafael. *Island Fighting.*
(Time Life Books, Alexandria, VA, 1978).

Sulzberger, C. L. *The American Heritage Picture History of World War II.*
(American Heritage Publishing Co., New York, 1966).

Terkel, Studs. *The Good War: An Oral History of World War Two.*
(Pantheon Books, New York, 1984).

Wertstein, Irving. *The Battle of Midway.*
(Thomas Y. Crowell, New York, 1961).
For younger readers.

Wheeler, Keith. *War Under The Pacific.*
(Time Life Books, Alexandria, VA, 1980).
The submarine campaign that virtually isolated Japan.

Index

Page numbers in *Italics* refer to illustration

ABDACOM 25
Abe, R. Adml. K. 46, 53, 60, 111, 130
Adachi, Lt. Gen. H. 90
Admiralty Is 89
Ainsworth, R. Adml. W. L. 71, 72
Aitape 90, 91, 116-124,
Akagi 34
Akatsuki 53
Akiyama, R. Adml. 71, 83
Alabama U.S.S. 8
Alamagordo 95, 112
Aleutians 10 (map), 33, 74, *75*, 85,
Arizona U.S.S. 12, 62-70
Atago 111
Atomic bomb *128*-131
Australia 20, 23, 27, 36-7, 60 (map)
Ayanami 54

Banten Bay, Battle of 26
Bataan Peninsula 10 (map), 19, 21, 22, 23, 24, 115
Belleau Wood U.S.S. *111*
Betio 79-*82*
Biloxi U.S.S. *7*
Birmingham U.S.S. 112
Bismarck Sea, Battle of 59-60
Blamey, Gen. Sir T. 60
Blissful, Operation 67
Bloody Ridge, Battle of 44
Boeing B17 Flying Fortress *49*
Boeing B29 Superfortress 74, 122-3
Bonegi River 45
Bonin Island 74, 126
Borneo 9, 10 (map)
Bougainville 40 (map), 58, *65*-72, 79, 88,
Brereton, Maj. Gen. L. H. 19
Bruce, Maj. Gen. A. C. 104
Brunei 106-7 (map), 111
Buckner, Lt. Gen. S. B. 118
Buka Is 64
Buna 55, 56
Bunker Hill U.S.S. 73, *99*
Burma 6, 10 (map), 24, 26, 74

Cabot U.S.S. 99
Cahaba tanker *121*
Callaghan, R. Adml. D. J. 53, 53
Cape Engano, Battle off 113-4
Cape Esperance, Battle of 49-50
Cape Gloucester 62-*3*
Caroline Islands 10 (map), 40 (map), 50, 74, 84, 93
Carpender, V. Adml. A. S. 59
Casablanca Conference 58
Catchpole, Operation 83, 84, 87
Cates, Maj. Gen. C. B. 104, 117
Cavite Navy Yard *20*, 24, 48, 50, 92
Cebu Island 10 (map), 19
Chengtu *99*
Chennault, Claire L *127*
Cherryblossom, Operation 71
Chiang Kai-Shek 8
Chicago U.S.S. 55
China 6, 8, 10 (map), 18, 28, 104
China Air Task Force *124*
Chitose 47, 113
Chiyoda U.S.S. 113
Choiseul Is 64, 67
Chynoweth, Brig. Gen. B. G. 24
Clark Field 20
Cleanslate, Operation 64
Consolidated B24 Liberator *124*-6
Coral Sea, Battle of 10 (map), 29-36, 55-6, 59-62, 65, 93, 100-*1*
Corlett, Maj. Gen. C. H. 83, 92, 95, 102, 108, 111, 115-6
Coronet, Operation 122
Corregidor 19, 24
Crutchley, R. Adml. 46
Cunningham, Cmdr. W. 17
Curtiss SB2C Helldiver *130*

Devereux, Maj. J. 17
Doolittle, Lt. Col. J. 10 (map), *29*, 85, 87, 122, 130, *30*
Douglas SBD Dauntless 6, *23*, *34*, *83*, *84*
Dr. Nagai *129*
Dutch Harbor 74, 96 (map)

East Indies 6, 10 (map), 24, 25, 26, 37, 73, 74
Eastern Solomons, Battle of 44, 47-9, 48, 51, 55-7, 79, 89
Eichelberger, Lt. Gen. R. L. 56, 94, 113
Ellice Is. 76
Empress Augusta Bay *66*, 71, 72, 88
Eniwetok Atoll 84, *87*, 88, 95
Enterprise U.S.S. 17, *23*, 28, 31, 32-4, 46, 50, *52*, 54
Erskine, Maj. Gen. E. 87
Espiritu Santo 49
Essex U.S.S. 73, 128, 131

Fitch, R. Adml. A. 30, 65 (map)
Fletcher, R. Adml. F. 29, 33, 34, 43, 47, 51
Flintlock, Operation 83, 84-*5*
Florida Island 29, 30, 42, 43, 46
Forager, Operation 95
Formosa 10 (map), 19, 40 (map), 104, 109, 118, 123
Fort Drum 24
France 6
French Indochina 6, 8, 10 (map), 50, 65, 72, 98, *122*
Fuso 111, 112, 114

Galvanic, Operation 80, 82
Gambier Bay U.S.S. 113
Geiger, Maj. Gen. R. S. 104, 119
Germany 6
Ghormley, Robert L. 42, 47, 49, 50, 117, 120, *121*, 124
Giffin, R. Adml. R. C. 54
Gilbert Island 76-*83*
Gizo Island *49*
Gona 55, 56
Goodtime, Operation 67
Goto, R. Adml. 49
Griner, Maj. Gen. G. W. *61*, 64-7, 70-3, 87, *92*
Griswold, Maj. Gen. O. W. 66, 59-67, 76, 79-82, 113
Grumman F4F Wildcat 6, 34
Grumman F6F Hellcat *22*, *52*, 65, 105, *107*, 109-113, *76*, *78*
Grumman TBF Avenger *31*, *80*
Guadalcanal 41-*7*, 49, 50, 53-*6*
Guam 9, (map), 17, 18, 102-*4*

Hale, Maj. Gen. W. A. 76
Hall, Maj. Gen. C. P. 46, 58, 60, 65, 75, 47(map, 64 (map)
Halsey, V. Adml. W. F. 28, 32, 50, 51, 58, 59 (map), 64, 65, 72, 88, 89, 103, 105, 106, 109, 113
Hansford Attack transport *118*
Hara, R. Adml. C. 46
Harding, Maj. Gen. E. F. 56
Hart, Adml. T. C. 19
Hawaiian Islands 9, 10 (map), 11, 17, 23, 28, 32, 36, 75
Helena U.S.S. 71, 130
Henderson Field 43, 44, 47, 49, 50, 53, 65
Herring, Lt. Gen. 56
Hester, Maj. Gen. J. H. 64 (map), 96 (map), 102-3, 119, 122
Hiei 53, 123, 126
Hiroshima *128*-131
Hiryu 34
Hiyo 102
Hodge, Maj. Gen. J. R. 109
Hollandia 90, 91
Homma, Lt. Gen. M. 19, 23, 24, 42, 44, 50, 51, 61, 71-*3*, 89, 97,
Hong Kong 9, 10 (map), 40 (map), 73, 102, 103, 106-111, 115-9, 122
Honshu 122
Horii, Maj. Gen. T. 55
Hornet U.S.S. 28, *29*, 31-4, 50, *51*, 52, 53
Hosogaya, V. Adml. 74
Houston U.S.S. 26
Hull, Cordell 8
Huon peninsula 60-2
Hyakutake, Gen. H. 44

Iceberg, Operation 118
Ijuin, R. Adml. 72
Imamura, Lt. Gen. H. 56
Independence U.S.S. 73
India 10 (map), 27
Inone, Maj. Gen. S. 106
Iowa class 96, *121*
Iwafuchi, R. Adml. M. 115
Iwo Jima 105-7 (map), 110, 116-9 (map)
Izaki, R. Adml. S. 72

Japan 6-10 (map), 19, 24, 27, 36, 37, 60 (map), 73, 74, 98, 106, 109, 118, 120-*131*
Jarman, Maj. Gen. S. 50, 51, 65, 71, 84, 96, 97, 102
Java Sea, Battle of 26
Java 10 (map), 19, 21
Jeep 62 41,
Jintsu 47, 72
Jones, Maj. Gen. A. M 21, 23
Jones, Maj. Gen. J. 24
Juneau U.S.S. 53
Junyo 53

Kaga 34
Kako 46
Kakuta, R. Adml. K. 33
Kamikaze *111*, 113, 114-*5*, *120*-2
Kenney, Lt. Gen. G. C. 59
Kimmel, Adml. H. E. 11, 17
Kincaid, Thomas 53, 112
King, Edward P. 23-4, 28, *37*, 40
Kinugawa Maru *54*
Kirishima 38, 54
Kiska 74-*5*
Kobe 113, *130*
Koga, Adml. M. 65, 72, 84, 93
Kokoda Trail 55
Kolombangara 66, 71
Komandorski Is., Battle of 74
Kondo, V Adml. N. 32, 46, 47, 50, 53, 54,
Konoye, Prince 74,
Kosaka, Adml. J. 56, 56-9, 72, 76, 81, 96-7, 101-3,
Krueger, Gen. W. 58, 107, 113-6,
Kula Gulf 71
Kure drydock *125*
Kure, Japan 31-2
Kurile Islands 9, 10 (map), 74
Kurita, R. Adml. 32, 72, 73, 111-3
Kwajalein Atoll 17, *18*, 83-*7*
Kyushu 122-3

Lae 59-61, 86, 90-1, 94, 96, 111, 116, 122
Lamon Bay 21
Landing Vehicle, Tracked *76*, *85*
Lee, R. Adml. W. A. 54
LeMay, Maj. Gen. C. E. 123, 127
Lexington U.S.S. 13, 28, 30, 31, *32*, *76*, *78*, *83*
Leyte 105, 106-7 (map), 109-115
Lingayen Gulf 19, 20, 21, 115
Liscombe Bay U.S.S. 79
Luzon 18, 19, 105, 106-7 (map), 109, 112 (map), 115, 116

MacArthur, Douglas 18-24, 27, 37, 40, 41-2, 55, 56, 58, 60-4
Macassar Strait, Battle of 25
Madoera Strait, Battle of 26, 119, 121
Makin 76-9, 47, 73, 76, 79, 82, 92
Malaya 6, 9, 10 (map), 24
Manchuria 9, 10 (map), 40 (map), 123
Manila 19, 20, 21, 22, 24, 115
Marblehead U.S.S. 26, 99, 110
Marianas Islands 9, 10 (map), 17, 18, 32, 40 (map), 60 (map), 74, 84, 95-9, 106-7 (map), 123, 126 (map), 127
Markham River 60-1
Marshall Islands 9, 10 (map), 17, 76, 83, 84, *88*
Marshall, Gen. G. C. 23
Matsuda, Lt. Gen. 56
Maya 111
McCain, R. Adml. J. S. 113
McMorris, R. Adml. R. H. 74

Merrill's Marauders *124*
Merrill, Brig. Gen. F. D. *124*
Merrill, R. Adml. A. S. 72
Midway, Battle of 10 (map), 30-6 (map)
Mikawa, R. Adml. G. 46, 53, 126, 130
Mindanao island 10 (map), 19, 20, 105, 106-7 (map), 112
Missouri, U.S.S. *121*, 128, 131
Mitscher, M. A. *30*, 83, 84, 98, 102, 109
Mitsubishi A6M Zero *109*
Mitsubishi G4M Betty 47
Montgomery, R. Adml. 73
Morotai 105, 106-7 (map)
Mt. Suribachi *117*
Munda Island 54
Musashi 112
Myoko 112

Nachi 74
Nagasaki *128*-131
Nagoya 130
Nagumo, Adml. 10, 13, 32-4, 46, 95-6
Namur Is. 83, *86*
Natib, Mt. 21, 22
Netherlands 6
New Britain 60 (map), 62-*3*, 64, 73, 89,
New Georgia 65, 71
New Guinea 6, 10 (map), 28-30, 36, 40 (map), 46, 55, 56, *58*, 59, 60 (map), 62, 64-5, 73-4, 89-95, 106-7 (map)
New Hebrides 42-3, 49, 75
New Ireland 60 (map), 65, 73, 89
New Mexico, U.S.S. 102-*3*, 52, 54, 59-67, 77, 79, 82, 87-8,
New Zealand 37, 92-3, 95, 99, 101, 106-7, 110-3
Nimitz, Adml. Chester 27-32, 37, 40, 58, 73-4, 76, 90, 93, 105-7, 117
Nishida, Maj. Gen. Y. 84, 87, 89, 107, 124
Nishimura, V. Adml. 111
North American B-25 28, *29*, 59, *64*
North Carolina U.S.S. 7, 49
Northampton U.S.S. 24, 53, 56-70, 74-9, 81, 87, 103

Oahu 10 (map), 12, *13*
Obata, Lt. Gen. H. 95, 115, 116
Ogata, Col. K. 104
oil 24
Okinawa 10 (map), 19, 105, 106-7 (map) 117,
Oldendorf, R. Adml. J. B. 109-13
Olympic, Operation 122
Omori, V. Adml. S. 72
Osaka 130
Ozawa, V. Adml. I 93, 109, 113-4

Palaus 106-7 (map)
Papua 60 (map)
parafrag bomb 123
Parker, Gen. G. M. 19
Patch, Maj. Gen. A. M. 45-*6*, 70, 78-9, 90, 122
Pearl Harbor 9, 10, *12*, 13, 14, 17, 19, 28, 32, 35, 105, 113,
Peleliu 105, 106-7 (map), *110*, 118
Pennsylvania U.S.S. 87, 89, 92, 95, 102-5, 109, 111,
Philippine Constabulary 115, 120
Philippine Sea, Battle of 96-*9*, 104
Philippines 6, 10 (map), 11, 18, 23, 37, 40 (map), 60 (map), 73, 74, 82, 90, 93, 98, 105, 109
Port Moresby 29, 30, 36, 55-6, 57, 93, 107-8, *122*-131
Portland, U.S.S. 53
POWs *130*
Princeton, U.S.S. 72, 112

R.N. Fleet Air Arm 10
Rabaul 56-9, *64*-5, 72-3, 88-9
Rendova Island *55*
Rennell's Island, Battle of 54-5
Rockey, Maj. Gen. K. E. 117
Rockwell, R. Adml. F. 74
Roosevelt, F. D. 23, 105, *131*
Royal Australian Navy 114
Royal New Zealand Navy 72
rubber 24
Ryujo 46, 47
Ryukyu Island 10 (map), 19, 109, 110, 117,

Saipan 95-104, 106-7 (map)
Saito, Lt. Gen. Y. 95, 96
Salamaua 59-61
Salt Lake City, U.S.S. 74
Samat, Mt. 22
Samoa 36
San Francisco 27
Santa Cruz 10 (map), 40 (map), 50-53
Saratoga, U.S.S. 6, 13-7, 28, 46, 72, *73*
Sarawak 9, 10 (map)
Sasaki, Maj. Gen. N. 66
Savo Island, Battle of 46, 77-89
Scmidt, Maj. Gen. H. 83, 96, 116
Scott, R. Adml. N. 49, 53
Seabees *69*, *71*
Seattle 27
Sendai 72
Sharp, Brig. Gen. W. F. 19, 24
Sherman, R. Adml. 72
Shepherd, Brig. Gen. L. C. 104
Shibasaki, R. Adml. K. 80
Shigemitsu, N. *131*
Shima, V. Adml. 111
Shoho 29, 30, *31*
Shokaku 29, 30, 46, 47, 52, 92-3, 95, 96, 102, 109, 116,
Short, Lt. Gen. W. C. 11, 17, 117, 120
Shortland Is. 53
Sibert, Maj. Gen. F. C. 109
Singapore 80
Smith, Maj. Gen. H. M. 75, 83, 95, 96
Smith, Maj. Gen. J. C. 80
Smith, Maj. Gen. R. C. 79, 96, 121,
Solomon Islands 10 (map), 28-9, 36, 40-1 (map), 42-*4*, 46, 47, 50, 53, 56, 58, 60 (map), 64-6, 72
Soryu 29, 36, 58
South Carolina, U.S.S. 47
South Dakota, U.S.S. 54
Southern Resources Area 6, 24, 109
Spruance, Raymond A. 32-5, 43, 47, 50
St. Lo U.S.S. 113
St. Matthias 89
Sumatra 26, 27
Surigao Strait, Battle of 63, 64 (map), 65, *68*, 80, 81 (map), 112 (map)-3
Suzuki, Lt. Gen. S. 86, 92, 96 (map), 107, 111
Swift, Maj. Gen. I. P. 90-5
Swing, Maj. Gen. J. M. 115

Taiho 102
Takashina, Lt. Gen. T. 104
Tanaka, R. Adml. R. 32, 46, 47
Taranto 10
Tarawa 76, 79-83
Tassafaronga, Battle of 54-5
Thailand 6, 10 (map)
Theobald, R. Adml. R. A. 32
Tinian 104-5
Toenails, Operation 65
Tojo, Gen. H. 8
Tokyo Express 43, 54
Tokyo 10 (map), 28, 126, 127
Toyoda, Soernu 93, 106, 126-7, 130
Treasury Island 64, 67
Trident Conference 73, 115,
Truk 40 (map), 46, 50, 56, 65, 72-3, 79, 84-*5*
Truman, Harry S 131
Turnage, Maj. Gen. A. H. 71, 104, 116,
Turner, Richard 42, 43, 49, 53, 64, 76, 95
Twining, Maj. Gen. N. F. 28, 34, 50, 65, 72, 98, *122*

U.S. Army 13
U.S. Army Air Force 65, 90
U.S. Army Forces Far East 18, 19, 21, 22
U.S. Coast Guard *63*, *87*
U.S. Marine Corps 13, 40, *42*, 43, 44-6, 49, 62-*70*, *80*-3, 87, *92*, 100-*6*, 115-120, *125*
U.S. Navy 6, 7, 13, 28, 46, 50, *57*, 107,
U.S.S.R 7
Ulithi Atoll *110*
United Kingdom 6, 27
Ushijima, Lt. Gen. M. 118

Vandegrift, Alexander *41*, 43-5, 71
Vella Gulf 72
Vella Lavela Island 66
Visayan 10 (map), 19, 23

Wainwright, Maj. Gen. J. 19, 21, 23
Wake Island 9, 10 (map), 28, 91
Waldron, Brig. Gen. W. A. 56
Walker, Capt. F. 72
Washington DC 7, 11, 23, *37*, 73
Washington U.S.S. 54
Wasp, U.S.S. 47, 48, 50-1, 54-5, 59, 123
Watson, Brig. Gen. Thomas 84,
Watson, Maj. Gen. T. E. 95, 104
Wau 58, 60
Wilkinson, R. Adml. T S 64, 106, 107
Wilson Brown, V. Adml. 28
Wright, R. Adml. C. H. 54

Yamamoto, Isoroko 10, 30-5, 50-*3*, 56, 65, 93
Yamashiro 73, 77-*9*, 84-93, 117, 125-6,
Yamato 32, *122*, 128, *129*, 131
Yokohama 130
Yorktown, U.S.S. 26-*7*, 28-35, *76*, 93-4, 124-5
Yudachi 53

Zuiho 52, 113
Zuikaku 10, 30, 46, 47, 113